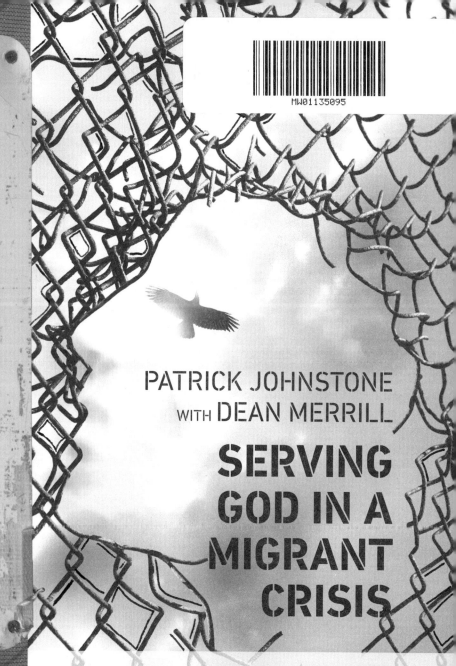

FOREWORD BY STEPHAN BAUMAN

PATRICK JOHNSTONE
WITH DEAN MERRILL

SERVING GOD IN A MIGRANT CRISIS

IVP Books
An imprint of InterVarsity Press
Downers Grove, Illinois

InterVarsity Press
P.O. Box 1400, Downers Grove, IL 60515-1426
ivpress.com
email@ivpress.com

InterVarsity Press® is the book-publishing division of InterVarsity Christian Fellowship/USA®, a movement of students and faculty active on campus at hundreds of universities, colleges, and schools of nursing in the United States of America, and a member movement of the International Fellowship of Evangelical Students. For information about local and regional activities, visit intervarsity.org.

All Scripture quotations, unless otherwise indicated, are taken from The Holy Bible, New International Version®, NIV®. Copyright © 1973, 1978, 1984, 2011 by Biblica, Inc.™ Used by permission of Zondervan. All rights reserved worldwide. www.zondervan.com. The "NIV" and "New International Version" are trademarks registered in the United States Patent and Trademark Office by Biblica, Inc.™

While any stories in this book are true, some names and identifying information may have been changed to protect the privacy of individuals.

Cover design: David Fassett
Interior design: Jeanna Wiggins
Cover images: caution sign: © PeskyMonkey / E+ / Getty Images
        chain link fence: © zbruch / E+ / Getty Images
        chain link fence: © kevinttawom / iStock / Getty Images Plus
        dead tree and crows: © zbruch / E+ / Getty Images

ISBN 978-0-8308-4535-4 (print)
ISBN 978-0-8308-7148-3 (digital)

Library of Congress Cataloging-in-Publication Data
Names: Johnstone, Patrick J. St. G., author.
Title: Serving God in a migrant crisis : ministry to people on the move /
   Patrick Johnstone, with Dean Merrill ; foreword by Stephan Bauman.
Description: US Edition. | Downers Grove : InterVarsity Press, 2018. |
Identifiers: LCCN 2018012241 (print) | LCCN 2018015491 (ebook) | ISBN
   9780830871483 (eBook) | ISBN 9780830845354 (pbk. : alk. paper)
Subjects: LCSH: Church work with immigrants.
Classification: LCC BV639.I4 (ebook) | LCC BV639.I4 J64 2018 (print) | DDC
   259.086/91—dc23
LC record available at https://lccn.loc.gov/2018012241

P 21 20 19 18 17 16 15 14 13 12 11 10 9 8 7 6 5 4 3 2 1

Y 36 35 34 33 32 31 30 29 28 27 26 25 24 23 22 21 20 19 18

CONTENTS

THE PEOPLE BEHIND
THE HEADLINES

When we hear the words "refugee" or "immigrant," we often think of political issues, not flesh-and-blood people. We emotionally distance ourselves from the struggling fathers, mothers, and children fleeing the violence of war or the scourge of poverty.

Stephan Bauman

But a heart-wrenching photograph that gained international attention in the fall of 2015 made the humanity of refugees crystal clear, at least for a moment. The photo showed Aylan Kurdi, a three-year-old Syrian child, lying face down in the surf on the Greek island of Kos. Aylan had died, along with his mother and brother, when the boat they and other refugees boarded in Turkey capsized off the Greek coast.

Looking at the photo of Aylan, still wearing his tiny shoes and a red T-shirt, we couldn't help thinking about our own sons and daughters. Suddenly, refugees didn't seem so different from us after all. Suddenly, grieving mothers from Iraq who carry photographs of their lost children seemed closer to us. We could empathize with fathers from Syria who keep their old house keys in their pockets as a reminder of home as they risk everything in search of a better life.

That's why it breaks my heart that such empathy is unexpectedly rare in evangelical churches. A recent survey of American evangelical pastors by Lifeway Research found that churches are twice as likely to fear refugees as help them.[1]

Why do Christians react this way when the history of our faith has been deeply immersed in the story of migration from the very beginning? Adam and Eve were forcibly displaced from the Garden of Eden. Noah was a migrant. Abraham, Moses, and Joshua spent much of their lives on the move. Jesus, Himself, was a refugee.

The Bible is clear about what we should do: welcome the stranger, or as Jesus called them in Matthew 25, "the least of these."

So where do we start? How can we meaningfully address our fears? What is God doing in and through the migration crisis? And, how can we help?

A good place to start is by reading *Serving God in a Migrant Crisis*. Authors Patrick Johnstone and Dean Merrill step into the fray with open hearts and hands ready to offer practical help. They grapple with controversial questions, wrestle with relevant biblical texts, present compelling data, and offer tangible ideas for getting involved. They are noble and trustworthy guides.

Almost every day I hear about a church, neighborhood, or community opening their arms to a refugee or immigrant family. These people are my heroes. Why? Because they have chosen to open their hearts, their minds, and even their homes to "the stranger." As they do, the language of "refugee" quickly fades away and is replaced by the words "brother," or "sister," or even "friend."

When Christians see tragedy in the world, we often ask God why He allows such horrific injustice and suffering. When we see a photo showing young Aylan lying dead on the beach, we wonder, how could God let a little boy like Aylan die?

Perhaps if we listen closely enough we might hear God asking us: "Will you help me bring this suffering to an end?"

Just a few weeks ago, I met some Syrians immigrants who are seriously reconsidering who Jesus is as a result of the care Christians have shown them. It would be a tragedy if other refugees were to reject Jesus because those who bear His name were too afraid to act.

As Christians who are part of Christ's Body, we have an unprecedented opportunity to seize a moment that could impact a generation or more. Now is our chance. We know we can do more.

Stephan Bauman
March 28, 2016

Stephan Bauman is President of World Relief, which empowers the worldwide church to overcome global poverty and injustice.

---

1. Lifeway Research: http://blog.lifeway.com/newsroom/2016/02/29/

PREFACE

GMI and I (throughout this book "I" refers to me, Patrick Johnstone) made our initial plans for this book on global migration way back in 2012. Before long, we realized that we're already living through a serious migration crisis.

Patrick Johnstone

Millions of people are on the move today—more than ever before in our planet's history. The world is undergoing a transformation, and Christians are wondering what to do. Some are rolling up their sleeves and getting involved. Others want to run and hide.

I have news for you. It's going to get worse before it gets better. Our world is full of war, poverty, terrorism, corruption, failed states, and ecological disasters, all of which uproot people and send them searching for a better life.

Today's migration crisis is here to stay, at least for the foreseeable future. We're offering this book in the hope that it can help Jesus-followers seek His leading as we walk together through this unprecedented challenge and opportunity!

Sincerely,
Patrick Johnstone
December 2015

THE IMMIGRANT IN THE MIRROR

If you're fortunate enough to have a roof over your head and a reliable income, it's only natural for you to think of today's refugees as "those people." You watch the news footage of coatless young men and desperate mothers clutching frightened children as they bob precariously in leaky boats or trudge along muddy roads . . . and you shake your head in momentary sadness at *their* plight.

In such moments, it is easy to forget that our ancestors may well have looked the same had anyone had a camera at the right moment to take their picture. The United States is rightly called "a nation of immigrants," but even we Europeans have to admit that nearly all of us arrived after the last Ice Age! I—though culturally English today—must not ignore that I'm the product of immigration. My Irish grandparents emigrated from poverty-stricken County Cavan to England in 1899, where there were more opportunities for a young doctor and his wife. They were not the only Johnstones to scatter across the world in those years.

And this wasn't the first relocation for my ancestors. They trace all the way back to an Irish tribe (the Scotti) that migrated to western Scotland starting in the fifth century, so that by the eighth century their culture, language, and even their name became the Scotland we know today. My ancestors settled in Dumfries on the northern border of England, and were *reivers*—a term for those who raided the English to steal sheep! Not until the seventeenth century did my branch of the family return to the land of their forefathers as part of the Ulster Settlement.

When the Irish Free State was established in 1922, my father gained dual nationality, even though he had been born a few years earlier in Britain. He always thought of himself as Irish, however.

On a skiing holiday in Lapland just before World War II broke out, he met an attractive Dutch girl. They decided to wed, and so my mother came to Britain as a "marriage immigrant." She learned English as well as she could, although my grandfather (in whose house they lived) always criticized her accent. Adding to her burden, she was cut off from her family back in the Netherlands for five years while it was occupied by Nazi Germany.

Eventually however, peace returned, and I got to know her side of the family. A Dutch uncle told me that, based upon his research, the family's ancestry tracked all the way back to a Viking chief who had raided northern Holland and settled there during the ninth century.

So . . . I have in me Celtic blood, Dutch blood, Viking blood—and not a drop of English blood so far as I know. When I look in the mirror, I see an immigrant. My boyhood schoolmates quickly seized on my obviously Irish name, "Patrick," and teased me mercilessly, even bullying me. To them, I was one of "those people."

The migrants scrambling today to reach our borders are no different.

■ ■ ■

At times, the subject of immigration has inspired soaring rhetoric. In 1883, Americans were trying to raise money to build a 155-foot-tall

I have in me Celtic blood, Dutch blood, Viking blood—and not a drop of English blood so far as I know. When I look in the mirror, I see an immigrant.

pedestal for the Statue of Liberty, a gift from France. They enlisted a famous poet, Emma Lazarus, to help the cause with an original sonnet. Her fourteen-line poem ended with the stirring words engraved on the pedestal's bronze plaque to this day:

> Give me your tired, your poor,
> Your huddled masses yearning to breathe free,
> The wretched refuse of your teeming shore.
> Send these, the homeless, tempest-tost to me,
> I lift my lamp beside the golden door!

But today, many citizens who live in countries that have seen an influx of immigrants aren't quite so enthusiastic about welcoming the "huddled masses" and the "wretched refuse." They see them as a drain on scarce resources and social services, as foreign influences that over time will dilute the national character, as even potential threats to security.

Here in this book, we're going to take an honest look at the various dimensions of today's migrant exodus. We will also ask what it means to follow the One who, while still a toddler, was a desperate refugee himself, swept up by his parents in the middle of the night and hurried off to Egypt to avoid King Herod's massacre. We will show multiple examples of Christians today taking action in their Master's name.

In so doing, we will echo the perspective of an ordinary woman who wrote the following letter to her local newspaper editor during a combative election season:

> He arrived in America by ship, unaccompanied and penniless.
>
> It is not only possible, but probable, that he was fleeing political anarchy, although famine and increasingly severe living and working conditions likely contributed to the exodus of which he was a part. He found menial work upon arrival, labor requiring scant knowledge or use of English. His understanding grew over the years, but he spoke little to none of the language of his adopted country. He and his wife raised eight children (all "anchor babies" in today's

vernacular) who became contributing members of society, three
serving in the U.S. military.

Should he have been "shipped back" upon arrival? Criticized and
mocked for his lack of English? Because he never became a citizen?
We'll never know since my grandpa died in January 1951.

I hear today's political harangues and wonder which of Grandpa's
anchor grandchildren these politicos would like to ship back to the
embattled and nearly impoverished countryside of the Ukraine. Many
of us have advanced educations; four served honorably in America's
wars. One of Grandpa's great-grandsons will soon enter his second
year at Boston University. So very far from the dangerous coal mines
of Pennsylvania where black dust entered every pore of Grandpa's
body. And soul.

Be careful, be very careful, you American politicians. Look carefully
into your own family tree. Be grateful for the grace shown to those
who walked before you. A wise first-century man once wrote, "The
tongue is a small part of the body, but it makes great boasts. Consider
what a great forest is set on fire by a small spark. The tongue also is a
fire. . . . It is a restless evil, full of deadly poison."[1]

With care—and hopefully with grace—we now turn to the dramatic
floods of people on the move across our world, what we need to know
about them, and what we might do on their behalf.

PART ONE

WHAT'S GOING ON

CHAPTER 1

A HUMAN TIDE

The distressing headlines and photos assault our senses almost daily:

DEADLY TRIP ACROSS MEDITERRANEAN[2]

RAZOR WIRE NOW GREETS MIGRANTS[3]

60 MILLION PEOPLE FLEEING CHAOTIC LANDS, U.N. SAYS[4]

DEATH BY SEA, LAND IN EUROPE—Migrant crisis grows as 71 people suffocate in abandoned truck[5]

HUNGARY CLOSES BORDER TO MIGRANTS—Refugees seeking asylum pile up on the Serbian side[6]

IMMIGRATION TALK STRAINS SOLIDARITY[7]

BALKANS: MIGRANT SURGE CONTINUES[8]

SPECIAL REPORT: EXODUS—The epic migration to Europe & what lies ahead (a 56-page array of articles, maps, photos, and charts in TIME magazine's October 19, 2015, issue)

At the end of 2015, the Geneva-based International Organization for Migration (IOM) tallied 1,005,504 migrants who had entered Europe during the year—more than quadruple the number of the year before. A million people. That's the population of the entire city of Birmingham (UK), or San Jose (USA), or Calgary (Canada).

Of the million, about half were Syrians; 20 percent were Afghans; 7 percent were Iraqis.

Drownings while trying to cross the seas came to 3,692, says the IOM (which is one-fourth *more* than all who died on 9/11).[9] Most memorable, of course, was little three-year-old Aylan Kurdi, whose red-shirted body washed up on a Turkish beach in early September. Pictures immediately went viral around the world.

Believe it or not, some 4,000 asylum seekers have even trekked through Russia instead, all the way to the Arctic frontier, to cross over into Norway for shelter. It means buying a bicycle and riding the last few kilometers in the frigid weather, since Russia does not allow buses or taxis to carry them—or even let them walk along the road. Still, "The road is safer," said one young engineering student from Syria trying to warm up in a Norwegian arrival center. "You don't have to cross the sea."[10]

WHAT'S AN IMMIGRANT? WHAT'S A REFUGEE?

Definitions to keep in mind . . .

Immigrant: Someone who has relocated (for whatever reason) to a new country.

Emigrant: Same as above, only viewed from the opposite end—someone who has left for a new country. In 1933, Albert Einstein *emigrated from* Nazi Germany. He *immigrated to* the United States.

Internally displaced person (IDP): Someone who has fled their home but is still inside their country's borders. (IDPs account for two-thirds of today's 60 million on the move, in fact.)

Refugee: Someone who has left their home country to escape war, natural disaster, or the fear of persecution based on race, religion, nationality, or political opinion—AND has been registered as such in a receiving country.

Asylum seeker: Someone who has claimed asylum under the 1951 United Nations Convention on the Status of Refugees on the ground that if they are returned to their country of origin, they have a well-founded fear of persecution on account of race, religion, nationality, political belief, or membership of a particular social group.

At the same time, as Europe struggles with the incoming tide from the Middle East—as well as Africans fleeing political chaos and terror—other parts of the globe are seeing their own waves of refugees. Rohingyas, a persecuted minority in Myanmar (Burma), paid unscrupulous people-smugglers to sail them to safety in Indonesia or Australia until that door largely closed, but by 2017 they were flooding into neighboring Bangladesh. Central Americans keep streaming northward to escape the cruel drug lords and ruthless gangs who abuse their homelands. These migrations don't garner as much news coverage, but for the individuals involved, each new day—and each dark night—is just as perilous and frightening.

> **Sixty million people on the move means that one out of every 122 people on the planet today is out of their natural home.**

National Geographic provided an enlightening global perspective in its set of graphics, "The World's Congested Human Migration Routes in 5 Maps."[11] These migration routes crisscross every continent except South America (and, obviously, Antarctica).

"We are witnessing a paradigm change, an unchecked slide into an era in which the scale of global forced displacement as well as the response required is now clearly dwarfing anything seen before," said António Guterres, the United Nations High Commissioner for Refugees.

Sixty million people on the move—that number is almost too big to comprehend. If so, then try this instead: One out of every 122 people on the planet today is out of their natural home.

Break it down even further: A staggering 42,500 people are uprooted *every day*. That's one person *every two seconds*. Half of them are children. Half are women and girls.

Just who are these individuals? Where are they coming from? And where are they hoping to land?

MY FRIEND REZA

Let me put a human face on the refugee crisis by introducing you to someone who has lived in my country since 2012, after being displaced not once but twice. Originally from Iran, he and his wife now work with a ministry called ELAM, discipling leaders for the rapidly growing Iranian congregations across the Middle East, the UK, and the rest of Europe. His name is Reza Jaffari. His story shows how God often sees more potential in refugees than we do.

I will let him tell the turning, twisting saga in his own words:

> I grew up in a Muslim family. I was born prematurely in 1983 on the birthday of the eighth Imam of the Shia branch of Islam, and was therefore given his name, Reza. In my first ten years, my mother took me 15 times to his shrine in the large city of Mashad to thank God for the miracle that I survived. We were encouraged to pray and fast and to seek God, but my sister and I were not forced to practice our religion.
>
> When I was 16, however, I had much earnestness for God. I started to pray and fast and had a passion for reading the Qur'an, gaining a measure of peace from doing this. My devotion did not last long, though; by the time I was 18, I started to smoke hashish and indulge in wrong sexual relationships. I was living a double life in which I was the "best" child at home, but with friends I was lying, drinking, and using drugs.
>
> At university I studied computer programming for three-and-a-half years, but my life went further downhill into addiction and darkness. I tried to pray five times a day, but things got only worse. Then came a bad road accident, during which I had a strange out-of-body experience. I saw myself going down into a pitch-dark pit. I could see nothing, but just heard shouting and screaming. It was a terrible feeling. Then I looked back and seemed to be floating above the scene of the accident, where I saw myself lying on the ground. Then someone slapped my face, and I returned to consciousness.

About this time, my mother and sister became Christians in a house church in Iran. They tried to explain the gospel to me. But it all seemed crazy; I accused them of apostasy.

In 2005, just five months after completing my university degree, I went with my mother and sister to the UK to join my grandparents, uncles, and aunts who had emigrated there some 40 years before. We wanted to escape the harsh realities of life in Iran. To get residence as asylum seekers, we invented a story to give to the UK Immigration.

My mother and sister soon settled into an Iranian church in West London, but I would not go with them. I managed to get a job. But after six months I was fired. Three days later, the church held a youth party organized by a friend of my sister, and she persuaded me to go along.

At the end someone said, "We know so little about Reza. Let's put him on a 'hot seat' and ask him some questions." It was really their way of communicating the gospel to me. They challenged me about statements in the Qur'an and fed me truths from the Bible.

Then one girl looked me straight in the eye and said, "Do you love God?" I said I did. She then followed up with another question, "Tell me one part of your life that you have sacrificed to show that you love God!"

I hung my head in shame, for I had given nothing. All I could see was my sinfulness, my lying and drugs. I began having trouble sleeping and had constant flashbacks to my dissolute past. The Holy Spirit was convicting me of my sin, and it was most unpleasant.

By the following Sunday, I was more than ready to go to the church service. The sermon that day was on the precious blood of Jesus that can cleanse from sin. It was a message for me. At the end of the service, a heavy weight seemed to crush me, making it hard even to breathe. I cried to the Lord, "God, I don't know you. I want to meet with you; show me!"

God spoke to me in that moment. "This heaviness is your sin," He seemed to say. I went to a friend and said, "I want this burden to be lifted. I need to repent."

He then asked me to repeat a prayer after him. This included the words "I accept you as Lord of my life." For a moment, this seemed to be going too far . . . but then the burden lifted, and I felt as if my whole body was burning from head to toe. I realized that He is God.

I had such joy over the following three days, hardly sleeping as I read and read the Bible. Amazingly all my addictions to swearing, lying, cigarettes, and drugs ended instantly, without any hankering after them again. I found out later that the Christians had been praying for my conversion all the previous week. So that day—11 December 2005—is very special to me.

For three years I became involved in the ministry of two churches in Blackburn and Liverpool. Then one day in a prayer meeting, God brought such conviction to me (and then to my mother and sister) about our deception of the UK Home Office that processed our asylum papers. I felt awful about living in the country on the basis of lies.

So we went to an attorney to confess what we had done and ask for help. It ended up with us being arrested on 11 December 2008 and sent to a detention center for 18 days—and then being deported back to Iran. Many Christians protested and made demonstrations to get the deportation quashed. It was well reported in the media, but to no avail.

On arrival in Tehran, the Holy Spirit showed me that I was now an ambassador for Jesus in Iran! Apparently He wanted us back in this place. Soon I got involved in Christian ministry. But when the Muslim authorities heard of it, I was given a stark choice: Either leave the country or go to prison. They did not want active Christians preaching the gospel.

So after just a three-month stay, I departed for Turkey (this being quite easy because Iranians can enter Turkey without a visa). There I was granted refugee status by the UN. I lived in Turkey for three and a half years and became involved in the ministry of ELAM. During that time, I met a young British Iranian lady named Shieva, who had come to minister in Turkey. She became my wife.

This created a new opportunity for re-application to the British Home Office, telling the truth this time. We settled in the UK. My mother and sister re-applied as well but were rejected; however, Canada accepted them, and they now live in Vancouver.

When I listen to Reza tell his amazing odyssey, I am filled with gladness. He and his wife are living illustrations of how "in all things God works for the good of those who love him, who have been called according to his purpose" (Romans 8:28). He is an asset to my country—and to the kingdom of God.

How many others in today's human tide are destined for genuine achievement? How many others will, like Reza, find eternal peace through Christ in the new places where they land?

"The migration of people, whether forced or voluntary, should be viewed not as accidental but part of God's sovereign plan," says Jenny Yang, a World Relief vice president. "With immigration, the nations show up on our doorstep. The mission field has crossed our borders and settled into our communities as our co-workers and neighbors."[12] Can we see the powerful potential—and not just the problems—in this unprecedented human flood?

ASK YOURSELF

- *What are your feelings as you watch the news of massive migrations today?*
- *How do you think Christ is feeling about all this?*

CHAPTER 2

HOW DO YOU *FEEL* ABOUT IMMIGRANTS?

When you analyze how we *feel* about immigrants, you can see that it has a powerful impact on what we think and how we respond to them. Often, our feelings come from our formative experiences within our families and communities.

When I was a small boy, I was the son of a country doctor in the west of England during World War II where we had few foreigners in our area. The only one I remember was an exile sailor from Latvia, a patient of my father's. He used to tell me some of his sea stories and also how he could not return to his native land because the Russians had seized it.

But once the war ended, and Britain opened its gates again to immigrants from across the Commonwealth, the scene changed dramatically. Hundreds of thousands of Afro-Caribbeans arrived—Jamaicans, Bahamians, and Trinidadians, among others. Before long, they were operating large parts of our transportation systems as well as the National Health Service in urban areas. These new neighbors were largely Christian in background.

Not so, however, in the 1950s, when Pakistanis, Indians, and Bangladeshis began showing up, followed by their countrymen who had earlier moved to set up businesses in Uganda but now needed to flee the cruel dictatorship of Idi Amin. These were all so different in clothing, customs, and religions—including Hinduism, Buddhism, Islam, and other faiths.

Every time I went to a British city of any size, I had to face the reality of my nation becoming multicultural. Eventually, fish and chips were no longer the national takeaway food of choice; the curries and tandooris of South Asia had taken over! By and large, the English people embraced— or at least tolerated—these cultural changes.

"After World War II, there was an acceptance for taking in displaced populations," says Susanne Schmeidl of Australia's University of New South Wales. "There was a finding of solutions. And now we have a couple of massive displacements with an increasing attitude of 'Go back to where you came from.' That, I find, is the scary part—how to negotiate that."[13]

> **Once World War II ended, Britain again opened its gates to immigrants.**

Even after the war in Vietnam, Western hearts in the 1970s went out to "the boat people," as they were called. The United States accepted more than a million refugees from Vietnam, Cambodia, and Laos, perhaps to help atone for what its bombers had inflicted upon that region for a decade. On a smaller scale, various European countries welcomed these exiles, too; France alone (the onetime colonial master of "Indochina") took in 128,000.

ANOTHER WAVE

Attitudes are different today. Now we have a whole new wave of "boat people" crossing the Aegean Sea and the Mediterranean to seek shelter in the European Union. How are they being received? What feelings are bubbling up as they arrive?

Viktor Orban, prime minister of Hungary, minced no words when in the autumn of 2015 he closed his country's southern border with massive coils of barbed wire—even though the refugees sought only to pass through on their way toward better job prospects in Germany, the U.K., and Sweden.

"The supply is nearly endless," said Orban on national television. "We can see how many are coming. And if we look at the demographics, we can see that these people have more children than our communities who lead a traditional, Christian way of life.

"Mathematics tells you that this will lead to a Europe where our way of life will end up in a minority, or at least face a very serious challenge."[14] He pointed out that if the refugees really only wanted safety from war, they could well remain in Serbia or one of the other Balkan nations through which they had been trudging. Their push further northward, to him, revealed their real goal: economic advancement.

Resentment in the United States—which has a hard-to-manage 2,000-mile southern border with Mexico—has exploded through such incidents like what happened in Murietta, California, in the summer of 2014.

Protesters blocked government buses carrying undocumented children and families to a Border Patrol processing center. Waving American flags and chanting, "Send them back!" the protesters forced the buses to turn around.

"We've had it," one woman told a Fox News reporter. "You can't come to our country and expect American citizens to dole out what you need, from grade school till death."[15] Donald Trump's promise to build a wall along that troublesome border with Mexico was a factor in his surprising election as President of the US in 2016.

The primary influence in today's setting often seems to be *what's good for me and mine.* No less than an academically trained author and scholar—Heather MacDonald of the Manhattan Institute, who earned a B.A. from Yale, an M.A. from Cambridge, and a J.D. from Stanford Law School—wrapped up a speech in early 2015 with this frank declaration: "Immigration policy should be forged with one consideration in mind:

America's economic self-interest. Immigration is not a service we provide to the rest of the world."[16]

WHAT ARE CHURCHGOERS SAYING?

Today, when researchers zero in on what people in the pews are thinking, they uncover large pools of apprehension about migration and migrants.

The respected Pew Research Center polled four groupings of people in the United States: white evangelical Protestants, white mainline Protestants, white non-Hispanic Catholics, and for sake of contrast, "secular" or nonreligious people. All were given a choice between two ways to complete the sentence: "The growing number of newcomers from other countries . . .

(a) threatens traditional American customs and values" or

(b) strengthens American society."

How would they respond?

White evangelical Protestants cast a landslide vote for *(a)*, 63 percent to 32 percent. The other segments were less lopsided; in fact, the secular respondents voted for *(b)* by a margin of 54 percent to 39 percent.

> Surveys show white evangelical Protestants are more threatened by immigrants than other groups are.

A few years later, the Pew researchers went back with another pair of questions: "Immigrants today . . . *(a)* are a burden because they take our jobs, housing and health care" or *(b)* strengthen our country with their hard work and talents."

Once again, white Evangelicals were firmly on the side of *(a)*, 66 percent to 24 percent. White Catholics were nearly the same (but not Hispanic Catholics). The "unaffiliated," on the other hand, were almost the exact opposite: 26 percent for *(a)*, 67 percent for *(b)*.[17]

When I read these statistics, my heart sinks.

Are my fellow Evangelicals so hard-hearted?

Are feelings such as these caused by bedrock nastiness and spite?

Or do the survey respondents not actually know any flesh-and-blood immigrants?

FEARS: REAL AND IMAGINED

I think it has more to do with *fear*, with concern that welcoming immigrants will result somehow in personal loss.

I admit that when I go shopping and overhear someone speaking Arabic or Urdu, I feel uncomfortable, apprehensive—even though I've had the privilege of traveling widely across the world. Still, a voice inside my head whispers, *What are they doing to 'my' country?*

If I'm driving along a street and see a woman whose head and shoulders are swathed in a *hijab*, my first thought is not "Oh, that's interesting." I tend to think in that instant, *Here's a person who does not want to associate with normal British culture. She wants to stay apart; in fact, she wants everyone to notice.* (Of course, it may instead be her husband or her father who is insisting on her clothing choice, I admit.)

In such moments, I have to make a conscious effort to reflect and possibly re-adjust my opinions.

FEELINGS, FACTS, AND FEARS

The worries people experience about immigrants are similar throughout the world. Here are the top five concerns people express.

1. "Immigrants will take advantage of our hospitality."

We assume they've heard of the various social benefits—free education for all children, welfare checks for those in distress, subsidized medical care, subsidized housing, and so on. Who wouldn't want to get in line for these things?

We tend to forget that as soon as newcomers start working, their payroll taxes will *contribute* to the nation's social funding. In the United States, one estimate showed that during just one year, *illegal* immigrants paid $11.2 billion into the Social Security Trust Fund plus another $2.6 billion into the Medicare fund—but they will never get to claim a penny of it.[18] Those dollars will go instead to shore up retirement and health care payments to legal citizens.

2. *"They may look innocent, but some of them have ill will in their hearts. In fact, their ranks may include secret terrorists."*

Granted, when I see a man with a bushy beard wearing a Muslim skullcap, how do I know he's not an ISIS "plant"? There have even been reports of young males dressing up in the full head-to-toe *burqa* of Muslim women in order to carry out crimes. That is one reason why some Western governments have actually banned the wearing of *burqa* in public—which has brought accusations of Islamophobic discrimination. The lawmakers insist they do not revile Islam but are simply trying to protect public safety. (Even United States banks sometimes post signs on their doors that read "No hats. No hoods. No sunglasses" in an effort to unmask any would-be robbers.)

However, when it comes to overall crime, the numbers show something significant. Michael Collyer, who specializes in migration research at Britain's University of Sussex, says, "Where rapid urbanization coincides with a significant rise in urban violence, migrants are often blamed. However, newcomers are over-represented amongst poor and marginalized groups who typically suffer the most serious consequences of violence—they are much more likely to be victims of violence than perpetrators."[19]

As for terrorists deliberately seeking to immigrate with the intent to cause havoc, governments are well aware of this risk and work extensively to neutralize it. Anyone wishing to gain asylum in the United States, for example, must undergo a laborious screening process that includes being photographed, fingerprinted, and interviewed face-to-face. Both the FBI (Federal Bureau of Investigation) and the DHS (Department of Homeland Security) are involved, checking and cross-checking their databases for any hint of danger. Dan Kosten, senior vice-president of United States programs for the Evangelical group World Relief, says that on the basis of his long experience, "If you harbor ideas to harm the United States, this is not the way to go!"[20] World Relief has welcomed and placed more than 200,000 refugees over the years—with no known cases of terrorists slipping through. The same cannot be said for Western Europe, where the flood of refugees from the Middle East and Africa since 2015 has overwhelmed existing immigration controls. Some ISIS-aligned "refugees" slipped in, and have been involved in serious attacks in Germany, France, Spain, and UK (together with homegrown terrorists).

3. *"Helping these people just increases the flood. It's all well and good, theoretically. But the more you help, the more waves that keep coming. Your generosity just swells the numbers even more."*

In a statistical sense, that may be true. German Chancellor Angela Merkel's welcome to Syrians has increased the flood from Syria (with a lot of Iraqis, Afghans, Pakistanis, Eritreans, and others jumping onto the Syrian bandwagon—or perhaps the boat!).

But anxious mothers and fathers do not live in the world of numbers. Young men who have been threatened with death if they do not join a certain militia or army are not thinking about global population surges. They only worry about the next meal, the next nightfall. Their personal panic leaves room for little else.

Granted, no country can afford to have completely open borders. Even Europe is re-examining its long-standing Schengen Agreement, which allows mostly free migration among twenty-six nations. Politicians will debate the rules, as they should—but for those migrants who *do* gain entrance, Christians must not treat them as pawns in a political argument. These are individual human beings made in the image of God.

4. **"They aren't coming for safety; they just want better jobs—and we don't have enough to go around now."**
The discussion about "economic refugees" versus "humanitarian refugees" has been going on forever. To try to make a sharp distinction is usually futile, because nearly every refugee is some combination of both motives. *Of course* he wants to get out of harm's way . . . and *of course* he wants to get some much-needed money in his pocket. It's nearly impossible to label him for one box but not the other.

Economic migrants have always made their way to Europe, to Canada, to America, to Brazil, to Australia and New Zealand, even to South Africa now with its relatively strong economy. That country is host to more than a million Zimbabweans, for example; one area near Cape Town houses 50,000 Somalis. Huge African populations already live in France, Britain, and now Germany and Belgium. A few incoming refugees, knowing that Europe might try to send them back home, deliberately burn their passports on the way so the authorities won't know where to return them.

But to us as followers of Christ, *does it really matter the motivation?* We don't need to sort out whether they're coming due to danger or joblessness, do we? Both categories of people need the gospel. Both groups are candidates for the love of Christ to be shown to them.

As Jenny Yang, vice-president of advocacy and policy for World Relief, says, "The migration of people, whether forced or voluntary, should be viewed not as accidental but part of God's sovereign plan. . . . We are called to 'make disciples of all nations' (Matthew 28:19); with immigration, the nations show up on our doorstep. The mission field has crossed our borders and settled into our communities as our co-workers and neighbors."[21]

5. "*They don't actually want to assimilate into our culture. Instead, they want to overhaul it to their benefit.*"

Again, there is some truth in this viewpoint as it pertains to certain populations, especially Muslim ones. In my country, we're having a huge debate just now over forced marriages—Pakistanis especially forcing their teenage daughters to marry a man back in the home country whom the girl has never even seen. The police are now cracking down on this practice.

We're also seeing a rise in genetic problems among newborn babies, traceable back to close cousins marrying each other.

ADDRESSING NEW REALITIES

Even before the November 2015 terrorist attacks that killed more than 100 people in Paris, the nation of France wrestled with how to address the challenges of immigration.

From time to time, France (with a 7.5 percent Muslim population) has seen riots, car burnings, synagogue defacements, and the like. One outburst was blamed on the police for having killed two Muslim boys. But further investigation showed that it had all been a plot: The boys had been sent into a power transformer to try to fuse it, thus raising a complaint against the city for lack of electrical service! Sadly, however, both got electrocuted—and quickly, the streets began to fill with protesters shouting, "Allahu akbar!" ("Allah is greater!").

The French authorities went to Muslim leaders and asked for their help in stopping the disturbances. The imams replied in essence, "All right, we'll help you—but only on the condition that an Islamic chaplain be placed in every unit of the French armed forces. In fact, you must pay for them to be trained in Saudi Arabia, and then pay their salaries once they return."

Did the government acquiesce to this bargain? Yes.

The German newsmagazine *Der Spiegel* reported regarding Duisburg, an industrial city of half a million:

There are districts where immigrant gangs are taking over entire metro trains for themselves. Native residents and business people are being intimidated and silenced. . . . Policemen, and especially policewomen, are subject to "high levels of aggressiveness and disrespect."

. . . Experts have warned for some time that problem neighborhoods could become no-go areas. The president of the German Police Union, Rainer Wendt, told Spiegel *Online* years ago: "In Berlin or in the north of Duisberg there are neighborhoods where colleagues hardly dare to stop a car—because they know that they'll be surrounded by 40 or 50 men." These attacks amount to a "deliberate challenge to the authority of the state—attacks in which the perpetrators are expressing their contempt for our society."[22]

I must admit that we Europeans have so far made a mess of the waves of South Asian and Middle Eastern immigration, and we're reaping the fragmentation of society along religious lines. We have to do better in the future.

And government decrees can accomplish only so much. Far more can be achieved on the personal and community levels, as people of good will and good faith reach out to immigrants with inclusive attitudes.

Rather than shunning them and hoping they stay inside their crowded apartments, we have the opportunity to invite them into our homes, our schools, our churches, and our everyday lives. There they can learn from us what it means to be part of this present culture—and we can learn certain worthwhile traits from them, too.

"The strength of our country depends on our acting in accordance with our deepest principles," a United States politician (former Maryland Governor Martin O'Malley) told a TV interviewer. "And one of those very, very deep principles—and it's taught in every world religion—is that thou shall be kind to strangers, particularly when they are fleeing death or famine. . . . We have to act like the good and generous and compassionate people we are."[23]

HOW SHOULD WE RESPOND TODAY?

When people face difficult new challenges, we don't always respond in the best way right away. We often let fear overcome love.

That's why we need to stop and remember who we are and who we serve. We are disciples of Jesus who follow the Good Shepherd of lost and frightened souls. That commitment should shape how we live and how we respond to the challenges we face.

The Bibles we carry to church assure us that "God has not given us a spirit of fear and timidity, but of power, love, and self-discipline" (2 Timothy 1:7 NLT).

Our natural feelings must always yield to the courageous Spirit of God. That's the challenge I face day by day. How will you respond as you face this challenge in your community?

ASK YOURSELF

- *What irritations rise within you as you see immigrants coming to your area? Be honest!*
- *If your new neighbors are immigrants, what actions should you take?*
- *Look carefully at 2 Corinthians 5:6-21. What happens when the fear of man (and migrants) is replaced by a fear of God?*

CHAPTER 3

NO END IN SIGHT

Some people tend to be optimists despite the bad news of any given day or week. Such individuals have managed to convince themselves that today's immigration turmoil will calm down in a few years.

They say the Syrian civil war—which has driven millions to leave their troubled country—will surely end: Either Bashar al-Assad will regain his supremacy, or the rebels will overthrow him and set up a new government with a modicum of justice for all.

They say ISIS will crumble once the world's nations get serious about fighting it.

They say the United Nations will rise up to its charter's high calling to "maintain international peace and security" and "[solve] international problems of an economic, social, cultural, or humanitarian character" (Article 1).

They say the new United States president and Congress that take office in January 2017 will gain control of the country's borders.

People can say whatever they want—but I predict we will see *more* migration, not less, during the next four decades. The main reasons are clear, as you will see below. My concern is with Christians who have convinced themselves that this whole migrant crisis is temporary and will quickly disappear, so they don't need to do anything about it. Early in

2017 I was invited to speak about refugees at an international conference in Europe. The title of the conference was "After the Flood." By implication, the massive influx into Europe of refugees over the previous three years was almost a major "one off" event. I shared my concern that there was no rainbow promise after this flood that it would not be followed by other floods.

It's *not* going to disappear in the near future, so we had better face facts and figure out what we can do to help.

A WORLD OF UNREST

Since 2007, the Gallup Poll has been asking people in 151 nations if they would *like* to go somewhere else. The answer may shock you. "About 13 percent of the world's adults—or more than 640 million people—say they would like to leave their country permanently."[24] The highest groupings of these are Chinese, Nigerian, Indian, Bangladeshi, and Brazilian.

> **About 13 percent of the world's adults—or more than 640 million people—say they would like to leave their country permanently.**

Their dreams are centered, as you might imagine, on getting to the United States (23 percent), followed by the United Kingdom (7 percent), Canada (6 percent), and other stable nations.

Large numbers of these people are going to do more than wish; they are going to get up and make the attempt to relocate. The European Union, having already absorbed nearly a million refugees in 2015, predicts another 3 million will come by the end of 2016. The very "capital of Europe," Brussels (home of the European Parliament as well as NATO headquarters), is already more than a quarter Muslim—and will be 50 percent by the year 2030, says esteemed sociologist Felice Dassetto in his book *The Iris and the Crescent*.

I am persuaded that today's flood of immigrants will continue for the next few decades. Here are the main factors why.

"FAILED STATES"

This is the term for countries that simply don't function anymore. Somalia, in the Horn of Africa, is one obvious example. Its government fell apart in the early 1990s and hasn't really been able to regroup ever since. Lawless warlords rule vast stretches of the desert and enrich themselves through piracy across the western Indian Ocean. No wonder frightened people want to get out.

Other examples of failed states:

Yemen, just across the water from Somalia. The Houthis—a Shiite rebel group—took control of the capital city in late 2014 and placed the President under house arrest. He fled the country in March 2015—the same month a coalition of ten Sunni neighbors (led by Saudi Arabia) came together to fight back. As one result, more than half the country's 25 million people are struggling to find food, and almost two-thirds have no access to health care, says the U.N. Office for the Coordination of Humanitarian Affairs.[25] To make matters worse, their limited water resources are no longer sufficient to maintain the population. Where will they go for refuge? By the end of 2017 nearly 10 million people were facing death by starvation in the ongoing civil war.

Libya. Yes, strongman Muammar Ghaddafi is gone—but in his absence, chaos reigns. In the meantime, the country has become a conduit for hundreds of thousands of sub-Saharan Africans desperate to reach Europe.

Eritrea is a major contributor to this flow, as many young people flee a cruel dictatorship and destitute economy.

Central African Republic (CAR). A Muslim minority managed to seize power, and the Christian majority reacted strongly. Some 400,000 people (of both faiths) were displaced from their homes. No wonder that when Pope Francis was there in November 2015 (the first pope ever to visit an active war zone), the president admitted her country was undergoing "our descent into hell."[26]

Guinea-Bissau on the west coast of Africa. It's a chief transit point for the drug trade into Europe. The government is almost entirely beholden to the gangs.

Democratic Republic of the Congo (DRC)—a huge land with astounding amounts of mineral wealth (cobalt, copper, diamonds), but with a government that can't control the nation.

Its neighbor, Republic of the Congo (Brazzaville). Yes, it has oil, but not a viable government.

And as everyone knows by now, Syria.

ON SHAKY GROUND

Other countries not officially in failure but tottering on the edge include:

Pakistan. The strong presence of militant Islamists especially along the border with Afghanistan makes this nation a special cause for worry. What if the El Nino weather pattern causes the monsoon to fail two or more years in a row, drying up the Indus River? The world could be facing up to *50 million Pakistanis* desperate for water and food. Where would they go? Certainly not to their eastern neighbor and adversary India. Their only recourse would be to head for the West (which they're already doing, mixing in with the throngs coming out of Syria).

Iraq. The comment made above regarding Libya can be echoed here. Yes, Saddam Hussein is gone . . . but is the country now safe and secure? Hardly.

Afghanistan. The Taliban considers the current government nothing more than a Western pawn and continues to wreak havoc across the land as NATO forces pull back. A large minority of refugees from the "Syrian crisis" are actually Afghan.

Mali in western Africa. Muslim militias in the north, well-armed by nearby Muslim states, have shown their ability to strike at the heart of the capital, Bamako.

South Africa. It pains me to add this name to the list, since I poured much of my early ministry years into this country. But I am not hopeful about its future. The present government is very corrupt and becoming increasingly unpopular, and the angry Left is likely to gain more power, pushing out the democratic, business-oriented side. Emigration among the white population could well increase.

Saudi Arabia? How long can the royal family hold onto its traditionalist reins?

THE SUNNI-SHIA HOSTILITY

Underlying the multiple conflicts in the Middle East and beyond are two "denominations" of Islam that show no signs of reconciling. They've been battling each other since shortly after Muhammad's death (A.D. 632), and in their honor/shame culture, neither side is going to back down. Iran, the center of Shiite faith, is determined to restore the pride of Shiite Islam after 1,500 years of humiliation. Now, for the first time in half a millennium, the Shia have military power (which they would like

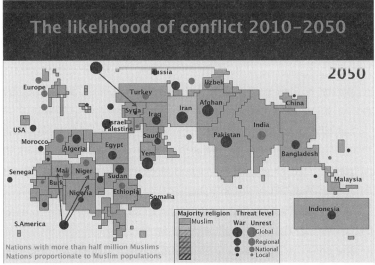

© Patrick Johnstone

to enhance with nuclear weapons). Nobody will be able to push them around—not even (Sunni) ISIS or al-Qaeda, which consider them to be heretical Muslims and even more worthy of death than the hated "Crusaders" (Christians).

This ongoing war will be a dominant feature of the next ten to fifteen years (see map), generating more waves of refugees.

The current battles in Syria, Iraq, and Yemen are but foretastes of worse things to come in other lands with significant populations of Sunnis and Shia, such as Lebanon, Afghanistan, Pakistan, and the Gulf States. It doesn't help that Saudi Arabia (the strongest Sunni power) extracts most of its oil wealth from its Eastern Province, which has a largely Shiite population! And of course, Iran lies only 150 miles across the Persian Gulf.

As long as conflict (this one or any other around the globe) rages, making peace and stability a faraway dream, people naturally lose hope. Their understandable conclusion is "Though I hate to leave my home, I really need to go somewhere else."

OTHER UNCONTROLLABLE FACTORS

In addition to everything we've said so far, there is the additional unknown factor of what natural disasters will come. No one can predict the timing or location of the next major earthquake, throwing masses of people out of their homes. If the earthquake hits not on land but under the sea, the resulting tsunami can devastate millions.

Drought is another unpredictable—not only for the Indus River Valley, as mentioned above, but in other parts of the world as well. If people simply can't grow their daily food, they *are* going to pick up and move elsewhere if they possibly can.

On the other extreme, floods may sweep away whole towns, ruining fertile fields for decades. A volcano can do the same.

The odds that our planet will somehow avoid all of these in the next forty years are small indeed.

THE MONEY FACTOR

You may have assumed that only the poor and hungry become refugees, while those with a bit more money have reason to stay where they are. That is not entirely true. The refugees pouring into Europe are, by and large, not destitute. They somehow came up with a thousand dollars or more to buy their way onto a smuggler's boat; once on European soil, they put out more funds to buy train tickets if they can get them.

Fraser Nelson, writing in the *Daily Telegraph* (Britain's leading newspaper), explains:

> This Great Migration was not expected because, for years, politicians
> believed that there would be less of it as poor countries became richer.
> Give aid, not shelter, ran the argument. "As the benefits of economic
> growth are spread in Mexico," Bill Clinton once assured Americans,
> "there will be less illegal immigration because more Mexicans will be
> able to support their children by staying home." When Jose Manuel
> Barroso led the European Commission, he made the same argument:
> third world development will tackle the "root causes" of the problem.
> In fact, the reverse is true.
>
> Never has there been less hardship; since Clinton's day, the share of
> the population in extreme poverty (surviving on less than $1.25 a day)
> has halved. . . . It might not feel like it, but the world is more prosper-
> ous and peaceful than at any time in human history—yet the number
> of emigrants stands at a record high. But there is no paradox. As more
> people have the money to move, more are doing so—and at extraordi-
> nary personal risk.[27]

Aid workers tell of meeting Syrian and other asylum seekers who carry credit cards and mobile phones. Their first desire is to buy a SIM card so they can call (or text) their families back home to say they have safely arrived.

Middle-class families in Damascus and elsewhere have been known to scrape up every bit of money from every relative—aunts, uncles, grandparents included—to send their military-age sons far away from the risk of getting drafted for this, that, or the other army. They can do better, with more options, than the truly poor, who can only walk to the nearest border and hope to get across. With money come possibilities for a whole new, more promising start.

FACING FACTS WITH FAITH

It looks as if massive numbers of migrants will be part of our life for the foreseeable future. All of this forces us, as Christ-followers, to recalibrate our views and responses to immigration in the 21st century. We have our work cut out for us.

ASK YOURSELF

- *Were you disheartened by this chapter's projections?*
- *How does this forecast push us toward more long-range planning and thinking?*
- *How can we better integrate a larger number of people from other religions as we go forward?*

PART TWO

WHAT TO
KNOW

CHAPTER 4

WHY PEOPLE RUN

Moving one's entire life to a new place is never much fun. Even under the best of conditions—plenty of time, plenty of energy, plenty of money, and even perhaps an employer paying the shipping costs—the process is wearying, unsettling, and disruptive. If you are relocating across a national border to another country, the task becomes all the more daunting.

How much more so for the person or family under some kind of pressure. Why do today's refugees make the effort? The answers come down to a number of *Push* factors that are forcing people to leave their homes as well as a set of *Pull* factors that attract them to other places.

PUSH FACTORS

Which factors *push* people to hit the road in search of a new future? The biggest factor may be *utter pessimism about the future.* They look across the landscape of their present lives, and all they see is war, corruption in government, and lack of economic opportunity. Will things get better tomorrow, or next month, or next year? Not as far as they can tell.

Discouragement sets in as people watch tax revenues (and foreign-aid grants) intended to build roads and clean water systems and keep them safe, disappear instead into the pockets of powerful officials. As just one example, Nigeria should be wealthy because of its oil exports (eighth largest in the world). Yet when the challenge of Boko Haram arose, its citizens were astonished by how the huge Nigerian army couldn't squelch this bunch of rebels in the forest. Why? Corrupt generals had stolen large sums of money intended for weapons.

Corruption is like having aphids in your garden. Aphids suck the life out of plants, so that almost no fruit is borne. So does corruption suck the life out of a community or nation.

As one *New York Times* reporter wrote: "Perhaps more than anything else, Syrians say, there is a sense of lost hope. One Syrian journalist describing his own feelings and those of many compatriots recently told me that they despair of a political solution to the war. Now, many suspect that even if there is a solution, Syria will not be a place where they want to raise their children—it will have grown more divided and sectarian— and so they might as well start a new life now."[28]

Conflicts of the First Decade of the 21st Century

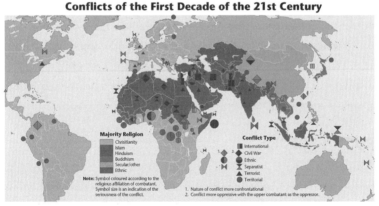

Taken from *The Future of the Global Church* by Patrick Johnstone (InterVarsity Press). Copyright © 2011 by Patrick Johnstone.

The United Nations estimates that more than 13 million children across the Middle East and North Africa can no longer go to school. "In some countries—particularly Syria, which once had one of the world's highest literacy rates—many children who ordinarily would be third or fourth graders by now have rarely if ever been inside a classroom. . . .

"In Syria, Iraq, Yemen and Libya alone, [UNICEF] said, nearly 9,000 schools are out of use because they have been 'damaged, destroyed, are being used to shelter displaced families or have been taken over by parties to the conflict.'"[29]

Adults, even without children to care for, face their own stresses. An Eritrean man now living safely in Britain was asked why he fled his country on foot.

"There were many reasons," he explained. "First of all, the national service [army]. It's compulsory and it never ends, unless you can bribe officials. You serve indefinitely—even 65, 70-year-olds!—without any salary, apart from pocket money. It's basically slavery.

"Eritrea is a dictatorship. There is no freedom of speech, freedom of politics, freedom of religion, freedom of press. There is no medical attention whatsoever. You can't go back to your home and see your family, so what kind of life is it? . . . The country is bleeding."[30]

Eritrea's dictator may not be Muslim, but he is vicious, and he favors Islam, which goes over well with his neighbors across the Red Sea. This is why so many Eritrean refugees are Christians.

The same is true for Iraq. As recently as the year 2000, Iraq was home to some 3 million Christians. Today, they number only a tenth of that. None of the powerful militaries of the "Christian" nations have been able to stop the exodus. The Assyrian Church of the East—one of the oldest Christian bodies—is being rapidly extinguished. This is just one example of this annihilation.

In the teeming refugee camps of Jordan, Lebanon, and Turkey, the Muslim populace is so aggressive that many Christian refugees are afraid to stay there; they scatter to the outside and look for shelter wherever they can find it, in monasteries, churches, or with local Christian families. This puts them at a disadvantage when well-meaning Western governments (Britain, for one) declare that instead of taking those fleeing into Europe helter-skelter on their own, they will welcome refugees from the existing Middle East camps. Under such a policy, most Christians end up at "the back of the line."

Of course, it's not politically correct in the West to report on Christians being persecuted. A lot of euphemisms are used instead: "intercommunal violence," for example. The secular press across the world just doesn't want to acknowledge this reality. Governments fear that they'll be seen as favoring Christians, so they end up doing the opposite. When Australia announced that it would take more refugees, specifically family groupings belonging to "persecuted minorities in camps," Muslim and human rights groups quickly complained that the policy was "discriminatory."

The world was more interested in the fate of the Yazidis, a small religious group that ISIS drove onto Mount Sinjar in August 2014, considering them to be "devil worshipers." The United States launched targeted air strikes to help them and dropped food and water from planes. Many were able to eventually flee to refugee camps in Turkey.

But then what? Thomas Albinson, the World Evangelical Alliance's ambassador for refugees, displaced and stateless peoples, explains what is true not only for Yazidis but many others across the region:

> [They] have heard about the dangers and risks on the highway to Europe. They have heard about untrustworthy smugglers. They have heard about drownings and death. They have heard about the walls and fences being built to try and stop them. They do not want to make the journey. But they are convinced that they have no other choice.
>
> It is up to us to create a better option for them.[31]

THE PULL FACTORS

What pushes refugees out of their homelands is not the full picture. The other part of the equation involves what is going on in the countries to which they head.

The most significant of these is the *massive decline in Western birthrates*. Fewer new babies means fewer school graduates down the road, which means fewer workers to run the businesses—and pay taxes, which help support the retired populations. Look at these numbers, remembering that a society needs 2.1 live births per woman of child-bearing age just to maintain the status quo.

The present economic model in many Western countries is not going to be able to cope with the aging population over the long term— especially at the high level of benefits they have been promised. The state pension in the UK, for example, carries the assurance that it will always stay just a bit above the rate of inflation. To make any adjustment to that would be a political nightmare; don't forget, old people vote!

Below is a chart showing the projected age segments by 2025 for two sharply different sets of countries: "AfAsLA" (Africa, Asia, Latin America) and "EuNAPa" (Europe, North America, Pacific). What will make up the serious deficit of younger people in the EuNAPa countries (the wedge on

FERTILITY IN SELECTED WESTERN NATIONS

Average number of children born per woman throughout the childbearing years (14-49)

Legend:
■ 1900
□ 1960
■ 2015

Necessary to replenish a population, keeping its numbers level: 2.1

Countries: Australia, Canada, Germany, Sweden, United Kindom, United States

the far right)? Not a campaign to encourage more child-bearing among the native population, despite how much governments and NGOs may try. The gap is more likely to be filled by those coming from AfAsLA (the darker wedge and arrow on the left) moving to new settings.

Incoming refugees are one way to keep Western factories humming and farms producing, at least for the present. No doubt this was in the back of German Chancellor Angela Merkel's mind as she welcomed Syrian refugees to her country. Of course, hiring and training those from another land with limited language skills can be complicated. They may be willing and physically strong, but they also need to comprehend the ways of modern industry.

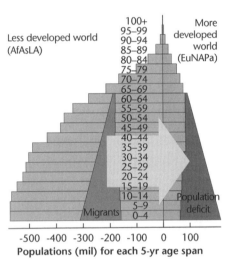

Taken from *The Future of the Global Church* by Patrick Johnstone (InterVarsity Press). Copyright © 2011 by Patrick Johnstone.

The ground-breaking United States inventor Henry Ford, father of the automobile assembly line, was a brilliant engineer but a poor student of people. It is said that he once rebuked his hiring department by saying, "Why is it you always bring me a whole person when all I really want is a pair of hands?" Today's immigrants are more than just "a pair of hands" or a strong back. They are complex human beings with traumatic histories now trying to find their way amid unfamiliar surroundings.

Much of the above dynamic applies as well to the nations of Japan and Korea, both of which are economic powerhouses but with low birthrates. What will keep Toyota, Sony, Hyundai, and Samsung running strongly in the decades ahead? Neither society has been especially welcoming to refugees so far, but they may be forced to reconsider as their labor pools shrink.

In addition to the West's need for young workers, other pull factors are obvious. Would-be migrants are drawn to the powerful magnets of:

- Peace and safety

- Better education for themselves and their children

- A living wage

- Democracy

- Cultural freedom of expression

- Freedom of worship, especially for oppressed minority faiths back home

- In short, the *restoration of hope* for the days ahead.

Adeyinka, a young Nigerian who spent 19 hours on the Mediterranean bobbing in a boat with 100 others before the Italian Coast Guard picked them up. He speaks for many when he says, "My plan [is] to be a learned man, to have a better future." Hopefully he will achieve that—even though his brother will not. He was among the 3,000 migrants who have died trying to make the same crossing.[32]

THE EXPLOITATION FACTOR

Our survey of why refugees run would not be complete without stopping to notice the shadowy characters who "help" them along their trek, reaping huge profits. Whether called "coyotes" (Central America and Mexico), "snakeheads" (China), or simply people-smugglers (Libya, Turkey), they get their money at the beginning—700 to 1,000 Euros per person—and if the boat capsizes, there are no refunds.

One doctor in the Syrian city of Aleppo turned to smuggling after "he ended up being hunted by both sides. The Assad regime wanted to find him because he treated wounded activists and rebels; the insurgents, meanwhile, decided he was pro-regime. So he fled."[33] When interviewed by a British journalist in a busy Istanbul café, he had netted 60,000 Euros in a single month. He could hardly answer questions, however, because his three mobile phones kept ringing.

Once a refugee actually reaches European shores, the Albanian traffickers often take over, working in concert with the Mafia based in Naples, Italy. They charge the refugee for transportation services and avoidance of legal requirements . . . unless they spot an attractive young female whom they can traffic into the sex trade instead.

Police forces can't seem to penetrate these gangs, because they are almost entirely comprised of family members, with draconian vows for secrecy and loyalty. Putting an infiltrator into such a tight group is nearly impossible.

To such operators, refugees have almost become a commodity—a stack of bodies to be moved from Point A to Point B for a price, like packets of cocaine. Smuggling people is actually more lucrative than smuggling drugs. And it's more secure; there's no physical evidence for the authorities to bring into court.

Meanwhile, the refugees are victimized twice: first, when civil war or another pressure pushed them to leave their homeland; second, when rapacious people take advantage of them along their journey.

When we see the heart-rending pictures of men, women, and children crammed into rubber dinghies on rough seas, taking on water, we must stop and ask, "Who owns that boat? Who bought the gasoline to run its engines? From where did it show up to collect these people? And how much did they have to pay?"

Even on land, there are entrepreneurs serving the refugee market. The city streets and roadsides of western Turkey are lined with vendors offering yellow life vests for sale. Others run a brisk business in forged passports and identity documents. It's a whole industry for those with an eye to make money.

One former lawyer for the U.N.'s refugee agency in Turkey says that the smugglers "know the local authorities and use them as a kind of protection." The profits get passed along to various government officials, even the military, "because otherwise it would be impossible to smuggle a person to Europe."[34]

The stern prophecy of Ezekiel echoes in the distance:

> "See how each of the princes of Israel who are in you [Jerusalem] uses his power to shed blood. In you they have treated father and mother with contempt; in you they have oppressed the foreigner and mistreated the fatherless and the widow. . . .
>
> "The people of the land practice extortion and commit robbery; they oppress the poor and needy and mistreat the foreigner, denying them justice.
>
> "I looked for someone among them who would build up the wall and stand before me in the gap on behalf of the land so I would not have to destroy it, but I found no one." (Ezekiel 22:6-7, 29-30)

Migration in our time is a messy situation, to be sure. But if someone is despairing enough . . . hungry enough . . . frightened enough . . . they will do just about anything to seek a better life. If they truly cannot make a living where they are, if they can't feed or protect their family . . . eventually they get desperate enough to go somewhere else.

Hopefully, someone will be waiting in the gap to truly help them.

ASK YOURSELF

- *After reading this chapter, what is your response to the common opinion, even among churchgoers, of "Refugees need to just stay where they are" (or ". . . go back where they came from")?*
- *What would you do if you were a Syrian or Eritrean today?*
- *What are some ways that you, with your resources and connections, can help lessen the effect of the gangs/smugglers/traffickers?*

CHAPTER 5

JESUS WAS A REFUGEE

"Historic."

"Unprecedented!"

These are the words people use to describe today's bigger-than-ever flood of global refugees and migrants. But people have been on the move since the very beginning of human history. The Bible tells me so.

Jesus was a refugee. So was Abraham. So was Moses. Jews and Christians have been on the move for a long, long time.

THE FIRST WANDERERS

"We need to move!"

The first husband to utter those upsetting words to his wife was not an Iraqi or a Somali. Nor was he a Vietnamese in the 1970s, or an Austrian Jew in the 1940s. Long before, back near the dawn of time, it was a farmer by the name of . . . Cain.

"Why?" his wife cried out.

"Because God said so," replied the exasperated firstborn son of Adam and Eve, who themselves had been banished from the Garden of Eden.

"He's upset about what happened the other day in the field. He said in so many words, 'You will be a restless wanderer on the earth' (Genesis 4:12). Believe me, I tried to argue with Him—I told Him that was out of proportion to what I'd done—I tried to talk Him down. But He held His ground."

Scripture records the result: "Cain went out from the Lord's presence and lived in the land of Nod [the name means 'wandering'], east of Eden." In time the couple had a baby; "Cain was then building a city, and he named it after his son Enoch" (Genesis 4:16-17).

The first human family migrated to a better place, and the human race has been following their example ever since.

> **The first human family migrated to a better place, and the human race has been following their example ever since.**

STRANGERS IN A FOREIGN PLACE

Over the millennia, a few people have moved willingly, but far more have moved under duress. All of them dealt with upheaval, inconvenience, economic struggle, and homesickness. Their stories show us the complexity of coping with massive change.

Abram and his entourage (including his wife, nephew, servants, and belongings) moved some 500 miles, from Harran to Shechem, because God had promised blessing in the new place. For a while, they weren't quite sure about that; a severe famine drove them another 300 miles to Egypt. They soon came back and worked through various challenges, including conflicts with neighbors, to build a new life. But it wasn't Abram's place of origin. "By faith he made his home in the promised land like a stranger in a foreign country; he lived in tents" (Hebrews 11:9).

His grandson **Jacob** had to flee after getting into a nasty clash with his twin brother, Esau. He spent two decades at their uncle's place back in Harran. Relationships were testy all around, until finally Jacob was able to reconcile with his brother and move back.

Things didn't go much smoother among the next generation, however. A long-running feud among siblings erupted one day, and the young, talkative **Joseph** was trafficked into servitude in Egypt. Soon he landed in jail on a trumped-up charge. He regained his freedom only when God gave him favor with the pharaoh.

Within a few years, another famine had slammed the land of Canaan so that **Jacob and his entire clan** had to migrate to Egypt for food. They ended up staying in this new place, finding work, growing their families, multiplying to the point of becoming a threat to the indigenous population. A new pharaoh tried to enact a brutal form of birth control, which failed. But even so, the Israelite nation realized they would have to move *again*.

Does any of this sound similar to the ethnic and relational challenges of our time?

FORTY YEARS ON THE ROAD

The lengthy **Exodus** of perhaps as many as three million people is one of the epic migrations of human history, the subject of dramatic films and Jewish ceremonies to this day. What must it have been like to trudge through the desert day after day, week after week, month after month, year after year? The ecstasy of escaping Egypt quickly faded.

Yes, they had basic food (manna) but not always water. Babies were born along this trek. The elderly died, were mourned, and were buried. And still the migration inched onward. The psyche of the nation was deeply imprinted, so that centuries later one of its most successful kings (David) would still say to God, "We are foreigners and strangers in your sight, as were all our ancestors. Our days on earth are like a shadow, without hope" (1 Chronicles 29:15).

Personal stories of uprooting and replanting pop up throughout the Old Testament. A young Moabite widow named **Ruth** left parents, relatives, and heritage to follow her mother-in-law to a strange place. Somehow she sensed that her destiny lay in staying with her mother-in-law rather than clinging to all that was familiar. And indeed, she ended up marrying, becoming a mother, and receiving the favor of the entire Hebrew community.

When the Northern Kingdom veered away from worshiping the one true God in the tenth century B.C. and "all the inhabitants of the lands were in great turmoil" (2 Chronicles 15:5), "large numbers" refused to accept the status quo. **"People from Ephraim, Manasseh, and Simeon** ... [came] over to him [King Asa in Jerusalem] from Israel when they saw that the LORD his God was with him" (verse 9). Their spiritual loyalty was stronger than their national identity.

In so doing, they escaped the dreadful exile that befell their country-men later—an "Anti-Exodus," so to speak. "The king of Assyria deported Israel to Assyria and settled them in Halah, in Gozan on the Habor River, and in the towns of the Medes. This happened because they had not obeyed the LORD their God, but had violated his covenant—all that Moses the servant of the LORD commanded" (2 Kings 18:11-12). The ten tribes found themselves marching the opposite direction from all they held dear.

> **Does God actually *cause* migration in some cases? Apparently so.**

Some 135 years later, it was déjà vu in the Southern Kingdom, which likewise had wandered from their commitment to follow God. "The wrath of the LORD was aroused against his people and there was no rem-edy. He brought up against them the king of the Babylonians, who . . . carried into exile to Babylon the remnant, who escaped from the sword, and they became servants to him" (2 Chronicles 36:16-17, 20).

Does God actually *cause* migration in some cases? Apparently so.

RUNNING FOR THEIR LIVES

One of the most dramatic, emotionally wrenching refugee stories in his-tory is this one, as recounted by GMI CEO Jon Hirst:

As I have been processing my response to the current crisis of people on the move, I've had a family on my mind. And the more I have thought about them, I realize that understanding their journey is the key to defining our response as the Global Church.

The story of their dangerous travels across deserts, along borders, and through cities is well known. I try to imagine the bags they hurriedly packed in the middle of the night to get out of town. The glances back at their home as they fled . . . danger behind and danger ahead.

Would they ever return to their home? What would their reception be like in a foreign place? Could they raise a family there?

Like I said, you have heard this family's story. No, it isn't a recent Syrian family walking through Europe or a Libyan family bobbing in the Mediterranean. It isn't even a Latino family making their way across the Sonoran deserts of Mexico.

I'm thinking of Joseph and Mary of Nazareth with little Jesus in tow. Why were they fleeing? Their plight came on the heels of the Christmas miracle, which turned into an unimaginable disaster. Once, kings had bowed down to their little one; now a different king had sent troops to kill that child with a viciousness comparable to what we have recently seen from groups like ISIS. Joseph and Mary wanted what so many on the roads of this planet today are searching for: safety and a better life for their child.[35]

We tend to gloss over the raw terror of what Joseph and his little family felt that night as they scurried away from Bethlehem. But if we put ourselves in their sandals, we will feel what refugees today are feeling. And in that, we will find our calling.

THE REALITY VS. THE LEGEND

The curious thing is that the further in time we get from a migration, the more we tend to gloss over the hardships and venerate the legends.

We tell stories about the "brave pioneers" who crossed rugged land and stormy seas for a better life. We build museums to their memory.

The most notable monument to the United States' history of welcoming immigrants is Ellis Island in New York Harbor, where some 12 million people from Europe were processed between 1892 and 1924. Today, it is said that more than 100 million Americans can trace their ancestry back to someone who came through Ellis Island.

The twentieth century, in fact, turned out to be one major migration after another. The post-World War I years saw some five million Russians, Armenians, Turks, and Assyrians driven from their homes by the Socialist Revolution and the collapse of the Ottoman Empire. World War II produced even more displacement of not only Jews but also many others across the European continent, forcing the United Nations to form a major assistance agency (UNHCR) in 1950.

> We gloss over the raw terror that Joseph, Mary, and the baby Jesus felt as they scurried away from Bethlehem, but if we put ourselves in their sandals we can feel what today's refugees are feeling.

On the other side of the globe in the 1970s, the Vietnam conflict forced some three million Southeast Asians to flee their homelands in boats, risking everything, much like what is happening today in Africa and the Middle East.

Back in Europe in the late 1990s, nine out of ten Kosovars ran from war heading for nearby shelter in Macedonia and Montenegro, until the EU could formulate some kind of response to provide asylum.

And now, here in the twenty-first century, the migrant tide continues unabated. It demands our attention, our prayers, and our action. If we don't know quite how to respond, we might want to reflect on the question Jon Hirst raises in the rest of his blog post:

Why did God allow His Son to live as a refugee? What purpose did it serve for the Son of God to be a foreigner . . . a stranger . . . an unwanted resident . . . an untrusted imposition?

In Hebrews 4:14-16 we see God's thinking: "Now that we know what we have—Jesus, this great High Priest with ready access to God—let's not let it slip through our fingers. We don't have a priest who is out of touch with our reality. He's been through weakness and testing, experienced it all—all but the sin. So let's walk right up to him and get what he is so ready to give. **Take the mercy, accept the help.**" (*The Message*, emphasis mine)

I love how Eugene Peterson's paraphrase captures the grit of Jesus' experience. Jesus suffered all that the refugees from Syria, Afghanistan, Myanmar, Haiti, and countless other corners of the world are facing. God had Him experience it all so Jesus could offer REAL help to the hundreds of millions of refugees who have walked this earth since He left it.

But how does Jesus offer real help today? Paul answers this through his passionate words in 2 Corinthians 5:20, where he labels us "Christ's ambassadors." With those simple words, the Church was commissioned to take Jesus' mercy and help to those who need it most. We are the ambassadors charged with presenting the refugees of the world with a Savior who has walked in their shoes and is ready to offer them mercy and help.

FROM "THEM" TO "US"

Today when you hear people talk about "the immigrant crisis," one word that's repeated over and over is "them." We think of migrants as those people. They're the "other."

But our brief review of the Bible shows that we are the immigrants and refugees. God's first people moved from place to place. Later on, Jesus had nowhere to lay His head.

Today, as millions of God-followers (along with those who don't believe) are on the move, we need to remember our heritage. God has used migration for millennia to achieve His purposes for His people. He is doing so again in our time.

Are we ready to play our part in this unfolding drama?

ASK YOURSELF

- *Had you noticed how often in Scripture people had to move— willingly or unwillingly?*
- *What is the history of immigration among your ancestors? Where did they come from, and why? How were they treated in the early years?*
- *What can be learned from studying what really happened in the last seventy years of migration waves? What did Christians do well—and not so well?*

CHAPTER 6

POLICIES OR PEOPLE?

As soon as the subject of refugees comes up, people naturally start talking about what *governments* should do. Elected officials are barraged with suggestions—and more often, *demands*—for policies to be enacted, quotas to be enlarged or reduced (or even eliminated altogether), border patrols to be beefed up, benefits to be reviewed. The average citizen focuses inevitably on how "they" should handle this challenge. Parliament needs to do this; Congress needs to do that.

Questions inevitably arise: Should immigrants receive subsidized medical care? Should they get a driver's license or other form of ID? Must they show basic proficiency in the local language? Under what conditions should they be allowed to hold a job? Should their children be enrolled in school? What if they want to bring more family members—brothers, sisters, aunts, uncles, parents—to the new country as well? What is fair to the indigenous population, and what is "taking advantage"?

The European Union's plan to mitigate the effect of refugees from the Syrian catastrophe by accepting 120,000 asylum seekers and spreading them out among the 28 member nations got vigorous debate. Four countries—Hungary, Romania, Slovakia, and the Czech Republic—flatly said, "no".

When President Barack Obama announced that the United States intake of refugees would be raised (from 70,000) to 85,000 (including

10,000 Syrians) for fiscal 2015-16—and to 100,000 for fiscal 2016-17—criticism erupted from many quarters. As soon as terrorists struck Paris on November 13, 2015, twenty-seven of the fifty state governors publicly balked at taking *any* Syrians, whether ISIS-connected or not. Noted evangelical leader Franklin Graham took to Facebook to declare, "If we continue to allow Muslim immigration, we'll see much more of what happened in Paris—it's on our doorstep. France and Europe are being overrun . . . ."

Canada, on the other hand, opened its doors with a smile to as many as 25,000 Syrian refugees in a three-month period. Newly installed Prime Minister Justin Trudeau showed up at the Toronto airport to welcome the first planeload just before Christmas 2015, handing out winter coats and saying, "You're safe at home now."

RULES AND REGULATIONS

Granted, every nation has a right to decide whom it will welcome and how many newcomers it will host. No one would seriously advocate completely open borders that anyone and everyone is free to cross. Just as homeowners have the right to determine who may enter their front door or whether smoking will be allowed once they are inside, nations are completely justified in defining residency and citizenship rules.

But such rules and procedures need to be fair as well as efficient, and that's not always the case. Shocking delays are evident all around the world. Here's an example.

A visitor to a refugee camp of 4,000 Yazidis in southeast Turkey in mid-2015 found these refugees had no formal status as refugees at all—the first step toward relocation. They "showed me letters from the Ankara office of the United Nations High Commissioner for Refugees (UNHCR), telling them when they would be interviewed to be registered as refugees. The earliest appointment we saw was scheduled for the year 2022."[36]

No wonder at least four refugees in this camp had already committed suicide in utter despair.

Latino applicants trying to "play by the rules" and enter the United States legally can languish up to ten years before their cases are decided. Once an application is formally filed and ready to go before an actual immigration judge, the average wait in the federal court system is an unconscionable 627 days.

It is therefore not surprising that so many Central Americans and Mexicans opt to sneak across the border instead.

The British system is equally broken, and the agencies responsible are failing to adequately control the flow of legal and illegal immigrants into the country, or to monitor them once they have arrived. This angers the average citizens, and brings misery to the immigrants. The UK has a relatively low level of unemployment in contrast to many European countries, so it is enormously attractive for both EU citizens (who are free to come and go as they please) and other foreigners (who face a tangle of bureaucratic barriers and delays to legal immigration). The issue of immigrants is one of the hottest issues in the country's political dialogue.

The Conservative Party campaigned for the 2010 election on reducing to "tens of thousands" the numbers of non-EU foreigners entering the country, but manifestly failed to deliver. As of June 2015, the total known immigration was 636,000 (1 percent of the total population), but there were actually estimated to be 1.1 million illegal immigrants living in the country in that year. Net immigration—allowing for subtraction of emigration statistics—was 330,000. Over 8 million (13 percent) of the population was then foreign-born.

We have a small, overcrowded country, and such rapid increases place great strain on housing, transportation, and health and education services at a time of serious government cutbacks to reduce national debt. The immigration crisis was one of the key factors that led to the referendum vote to leave the European Union in June 2016, and also could lead to the demise of the Union itself.

Whatever our nationality, citizens who care about justice for the "alien and stranger" need to work to reform these policies and practices.

After all, 99 percent of the world's refugees are *not* being safely resettled, whether inside the borders of their own country, in a nearby country, or across an ocean.

Instead, they are waiting, waiting, waiting, often in squalid conditions as the months and years tick by.

REAL PEOPLE

For the Christian, there is a deeper level in all this than laws and legalities. Dr. M. Daniel Carroll Rodas, professor of Old Testament at Wheaton College and author of the book *Christians at the Border: Immigration, the Church, and the Bible* (Brazos, 2013), says that too often "the conversation [about immigrants] seems to start with *legal status*. Maybe we ought to begin with their *humanity*—people made in the image of God."[37]

(For Dr. Carroll, the subject is not just academic; his father is American, although the son of Irish immigrants, while his mother is Guatemalan. At six feet six inches tall, he jokes that he's "the tallest Guatemalan you'll ever meet." He taught in a Guatemala City seminary for 15 years.)

> "The conversation [about immigrants] seems to start with *legal status*. Maybe we ought to begin with their *humanity*—people made in the image of God."

We must never become so enmeshed in the politics of immigration that we stop seeing the real, living, breathing men and women, boys and girls who are at the center of the debate. These are individual people for whom Christ died. He still loves them, watches over them, and sees their anxiety and suffering.

David Roller, a former missionary and now a bishop in the Free Methodist Church, tells about a flash of insight that struck him in this regard:

I was standing on a street corner in Asia when I realized that nearly everyone else was wearing flip-flops. I stood there in my brown Rockports, clearly an oddball, albeit a well-shod oddball. . . .

I stood there reflecting that there is a flip-flop world that is overpopulated and hungry, while there's a closed-toe-shoe world that is depopulating and overfed. The flip-flop world battles for daily survival. The smaller world of shoes frets about retirement plans.

The edges of the collision between those two worlds are called immigration.

Bishop Roller then goes on to apply the metaphor to our conversations about refugees:

For Christians, there are two interwoven matters here: one called "immigration," the other "immigrants." The former is about economic policy; the latter is about people. The former is about a country's right to establish laws; the latter is about the treatment of people, especially undocumented immigrants. . . .

But those two tensions are not made of the same moral stuff. The Christian's care for people operates on a higher moral plane than the Christian's concern for economic policy. This higher plane is established in the gospel where we discover the dignity of every person and the presence of the Lord, who made Himself one with the immigrants when He said, "I was a stranger and you welcomed me" (Matthew 25:35).

Consequently, followers of this "stranger" named Jesus are distinguished by their disproportionate care for other strangers in their communities.[38]

In later chapters of this book we will explore in greater depth the various ways and means that Christians are employing to affect the lives of real immigrants. Governments are free to make whatever laws and policies they wish. Meanwhile, the Body of Christ must also exercise its freedom to come alongside those who need safety, sustenance, and the Good News.

For four years after the start of the Syrian civil war, I spoke at conferences on immigrants about the impending crisis of immigration from Syria, and I declared that we in Europe would need to be ready to receive a million refugees. It took some time for this to become the crisis of 2015, but even my dire prediction was too small for the flood of Syrian refugees coming across the Mediterranean and Aegean.

It was Angela Merkel, Germany's Chancellor, who welcomed them—in contrast to many other European nations. The British government, I am sorry to say, refused to help until they realized the swell of public opinion, both Christian and non-Christian, to show more mercy to these hapless refugees. However the 20,000 refugees the UK agreed to welcome by the year 2020 bears little comparison to the 3,000-5,000 *a day* landing in Greece during 2015.

WHO ACTUALLY CARES?

Below the surface of politics are important moral issues, says Benjamin Wittes, a senior fellow at the prestigious Brookings Institution in Washington, D.C. (what one university calls "the most influential think tank in the world"):

> The tens of thousands of people [whom] governors are pledging to keep out of their states are . . . innocent victims of the very people we are fighting. Nobody contests this. . . . The concern, rather, is that some tiny percentage of them will be sleeper operatives infiltrated into a much larger group of people deserving of our protection.
>
> I would make an analogy here to throwing out babies with bathwater, except that it would be in poor taste. We're dealing with real babies, after all.

Wittes says we need strategic wisdom to help us figure out if it's *smart* to turn our backs on the refugee masses. (His comments are just as relevant to Europe and Australasia as they are to North America.)

> Imagine teeming refugee camps in which everyone knows that
> America has abandoned them. Imagine the conspiracy theories that
> will be rife in those camps. Imagine the terrorist groups that will
> recruit from them and the righteous case they will make about how,
> for all its talk, the United States left Syria to burn and Syrians to
> live in squalor in wretched camps in neighboring countries. I don't
> know if this situation is more dangerous, less dangerous, or about as
> dangerous as the situation in which we admit a goodly number of
> refugees, help resettle others, and run some risk—which we endeavor
> to mitigate—that we might admit some bad guys. But this is not a
> situation in which all of the risk is stacked on the side of doing good,
> while turning away is the safe option. This is risk whatever we do or
> don't do.
>
> Most profoundly, there is risk associated with saying loudly and
> unapologetically that we don't care what happens to hundreds of
> thousands of innocent people—or that we care if they're Christian but
> not if they're Muslim, or that we care but we'll keep them out anyway
> if there's even a fraction of a percent chance they are not what they
> claim to be. They hear us when we say these things. And they will see
> what we do. And those things too have security consequences.[39]

To be a Christian is to care and to act. Even in the Old Testament era, when God's plan called for Israel to be a unique, distinct society in the earth—the Chosen People—his prophets did not dismiss the needs of outsiders. In a time of severe national trouble, with a crumbling economy and major pressure from enemy armies, Jeremiah was nonetheless sent to tell the king of Judah, "This is what the LORD says: Do what is just and right. *Rescue from the hand of the oppressor the one who has been robbed. Do no wrong or violence to the foreigner, the fatherless or the widow,* and do not shed innocent blood in this place" (Jeremiah 22:3, emphasis added).

Several hundred years later, the prophet Malachi reinforced God's passion about this issue:

> *"So I will come to put you on trial. I will be quick to testify against . . . those who defraud laborers of their wages, who oppress the widows and the fatherless, and deprive the foreigners among you of justice, but do not fear me," says the* LORD *Almighty.* (Malachi 3:5, emphasis added).

Let it never be said that we "would have liked to" help today's refugees, but the policy environment was not conducive, and so we turned to other activities. "Of course we want to keep terrorists out of our country," says Leith Anderson, president of the National Association of Evangelicals (United States) "but let's not punish the victims of ISIS for the sins of ISIS."[40]

His colleague Matthew Soerens, United States director of church mobilization for World Relief, adds, "With the government doing its job of screening and vetting, our role can't be to ask, 'Is this safe?' We have to ask, 'Who is my neighbor?'"[41]

The needs of real people—God's highest creation—must always trump political arguments and personal fear.

ASK YOURSELF

- *What does Scripture require of you that goes beyond civic duty?*
- *Is your country's immigration policy fair and just? If not, what aspects need to be changed?*
- *How can you and your fellow Christians influence government policy with regard to immigration?*

CHAPTER 7

THE BLESSINGS OF IMMIGRATION

Amid the news flood of dramatic, heart-rending pictures—mothers clutching babies as they stumble across muddy fields, shirtless boys swimming toward rocky shorelines, weary grandmothers huddling under blue tarpaulins waiting for aid—it is easy to assume that this is the essence of immigration in our time.

But as the old saying goes, looks can be deceiving. Single snapshots and 20-second video clips do not tell the whole story of what lies ahead for people on the move. If we could revisit these individuals a year later, or two, or five, we might see a much better outlook. If we could track what their children become in the new place, we might have cause for genuine congratulations.

Taking the wider view would compel us to recognize two powerful benefits of immigration that are often overlooked in the heat of political battle.

IMMIGRATION CAN RE-ENERGIZE A COMPLACENT SOCIETY

Whenever a diaspora emerges in a new place as a functioning community, they are liberated from the restrictions of their homeland. They often thrive and do better than even the local population.

Why is this? Because they know they have to struggle to survive. They instinctively support one another.

They don't expect favors. They bring a work ethic that is often higher than those around them. They know they're starting from behind and have to catch up.

The African contribution to Europe has been extraordinary. The Nigerians, especially, are comfortable in their own personalities. Yes, some Englishmen may find them a bit brash, but they are making a contribution and rising rapidly. Over time, they have become doctors, lawyers, scientists, and even judges in our courts. (Many of them, incidentally, are fine Christians. But we see equal advances among the immigrant Hindus and Sikhs.)

The same has proven true of the South Asians who in 1972 were booted out of Uganda by the dictator Idi Amin. They had been the main traders of the country—and suddenly with just 90 days' notice, they had to leave. It caused great havoc there. But now, a generation later, they have done very well in Britain, not only in commerce but also in the professions. Many of them are part of the upper middle class.

Further back, we had a huge immigration of Irish during the Great Famine of the 1840s. They couldn't find many jobs other than being "carters," hauling goods from one place to another. In time, however, they came to dominate the trucking industry.

The same dynamic holds true for the United States. Dr. Joseph Castleberry, president of a Christian university in the Seattle area, has written a book called *The New Pilgrims: How Immigrants Are Renewing America's Faith and Values.*

"Today's immigrants to America champion the values of the Pilgrims who landed at Plymouth Rock in 1620," writes Castleberry. "They have a vision for personal opportunity and spiritual exceptionalism that come together in greatness for the noble nation they have come to help build."[42]

Speaking with a Fox News interviewer, Castleberry added, "If you look back at America's history, immigrants have always been a source for the renewal of our deepest values. Immigrants have always come to America looking for an opportunity, they tend to come with a strong religious faith, they tend to be moral people who work hard . . . . They not only become Americans themselves, they help America continue to be the nation its founders envisioned."[43]

Commentator John Stossel, a self-described libertarian, argues frankly that "Immigrants bring us new ideas. They invent more things than native-born Americans. . . . Immigrants from Nigeria, Jamaica and Ghana are more likely to be employed than native-born Americans and twice as likely to get a college degree. . . . The facts show that immigration is mostly good."[44]

> **Americans should remember that some of their most respected leaders were foreign-born.**

People in the United States would do well to recall the national leaders who were foreign-born:

- Alexander Hamilton, Founding Father and familiar face on the ten-dollar bill (born out of wedlock on the Caribbean island of Nevis; later orphaned; came to New Jersey for schooling at age 17).

- Felix Frankfurter, associate justice of the Supreme Court for a quarter century (born in Austria; came with his Jewish family at age 12).

- Madeleine Albright, first female Secretary of State (born in Czechoslovakia; fled to England during World War II, finally arrived with her parents at Ellis Island as an 11-year-old).

- S. I. Hayakawa, renowned linguist, psychologist, university president, and United States Senator (born to Japanese immigrant parents living in Canada; came to the United States after completing graduate school).

- Antonia Coello Novello, first female Surgeon General (born in Puerto Rico; came to the mainland only after earning her M.D. degree).

- Samantha Power, US Ambassador to the United Nations, 2013–2017 (born in Ireland; came with her parents at age nine).

Who gave us the search engine, Google? Two young Stanford University students, one of whom was Sergey Brin—born in Moscow, and brought to the United States at age six.

Who gave us YouTube? Three early employees of PayPal, two of whom were Steve Chen (born in Taiwan, came to the United States at age 15) and Jawed Karim (of Bangladeshi descent, born in East Germany, came to the United States as a teenager).

Who gave us the ATM machine? Luther George Simjian, born in today's Turkey near the Syrian border (the scene of much fighting in our time). During the Armenian Genocide, he got separated from his Armenian family and finally wound up in the United States at age 15.

Who sewed the first pair of blue jeans? A tailor from Latvia named Jacob Davis, who had immigrated to the States at 23 and was working for the now-world-famous Levi Strauss—who himself had left his native Germany to come to New York City at age 18, eventually setting up shop in San Francisco.

Many other examples could be cited from many settings around the globe. Not all of them captured national headlines as these did. They have made their mark in positive ways on the cities and towns where they settled.

There's a further dynamic of immigration that demands our attention: the faith factor.

IMMIGRATION CAN RE-ENERGIZE A COMPLACENT FAITH

At the European Diaspora Conference in 2013, I listened to a presentation by Willi Ferderer, a German Evangelical leader. He told us that in his country with 2.4 million Evangelicals, fully one-third of them (800,000) are immigrants!

The average citizen in the West thinks, *All these immigrants coming from the Middle East—they're all Muslims.* No, they're not. The arriving Christians don't stand out visually the way many Muslims do as they continue wearing Islamic dress. But they are our brothers and sisters in Christ. In fact, the rate of emigration is higher for the indigenous

Christian population because the rise of Islamic extremism has greatly increased the persecution of these Christians, leading to a tragic reduction of the historic Christian population of the region.

The immigrant believers are actually bolstering some of the declining evangelical populations in the lands where they go. Some denominations are rapidly becoming multiethnic.

"If you go to the largest church in Europe," writes Paul Borthwick, "you'll find it pastored by a Nigerian missionary. The largest church in London is pastored by a Nigerian missionary, and one of the five largest churches in New York City is pastored by a Nigerian missionary."[45]

Mission agencies are finding that the "one-and-a-half generation" (those who were brought to a new land as children and quickly became Westernized) are the most valuable and enthusiastic recruits to take the gospel back to their ancestral homelands, or even elsewhere. They are already bicultural. Often they know several languages. A prime example of this: the South Korean missionary force, now one of the largest and most vigorous in the world.

Americans sometimes assume that Arab-Americans in their midst are uniformly Muslim. Not true! Of the 5 million Arabs residing in the United States, two-thirds of them have a Christian heritage. Many of them, or their parents, actually fled from countries that were hostile to their faith. They came hoping to be welcomed by their fellow believers.

> **Of the 5 million Arabs residing in the United States, two-thirds of them have a Christian heritage.**

Philip Jenkins, the Welsh scholar (now teaching at Baylor University in the United States) opened many eyes with his book *The Next Christendom* (2002) and its sequels. Jenkins has written a book specifically about Europe, entitled *God's Continent* (2007). Says one reviewer: "He points out that when people assume that Europe will become exceedingly Muslim, they forget that a large number of immigrants coming into Europe from other African countries are Christians fleeing Islam."[46]

When desperate migrants first began pouring out of Libya in rubber boats toward Italy, the mission I serve (WEC—Worldwide Evangelization for Christ) quickly mustered response teams that could speak Arabic . . . only to discover upon arriving in the region that most of the refugees weren't Libyan Muslims at all. They were coming from other African nations, speaking other languages (including English)—and many of them professed Christianity. In the subsequent five years, the flow of Africans has massively increased. At the end of 2017 it was estimated that nearly one million sub-Saharan Africans were making their way north, hoping to cross the Mediterranean Sea into Europe.

One of our WEC leaders, a Moroccan, predicts a huge implosion within Islam. "Millions across North Africa and into the Middle East are pulling back from anything to do with Islam," he says. "They're becoming secular, or even Christian." All of this says to us Westerners that if we handle the immigration crisis aright, there could be enormous positives for the future.

My research into BMBs (believers from a Muslim background) shows the following remarkable growth patterns:

The growth of BMB numbers since 1960

The top line shows the worldwide increase, despite (or in response to?) certain political upheavals. The surge in Indonesia (the world's largest Muslim nation) has been especially dramatic. But even if we remove those numbers, the remaining nations (the lower line) show a steady upward trajectory, especially since the 1990s. What nations are these? Here is a list:

1960		**2000**		**2010**	
Indonesia	40,000	Indonesia	4,500,000	Indonesia	6,500,000
Nigeria	30,000	Nigeria	400,000	Nigeria	600,000
United States	30,000	United States	230,000	United States	450,000
Tanzania	20,000	Tanzania	130,000	Ethiopia	400,000
Ghana	10,000	Bangladesh	35,000	Algeria	380,000
Kenya	10,000	Iran	30,000	Iran	350,000
Egypt	5,000	Saudi Arabia	30,000	Burkina Faso	200,000
Uganda	5,000	Canada	27,000	Tanzania	180,000
Cameroon	3,000	Kenya	25,000	Georgia	161,300
France	2,200	Bulgaria	25,000	Bangladesh	130,000
Australia	2,000	Uganda	24,000	Cameroon	90,000
Benin	2,000	Cameroon	20,000	Kenya	70,000
Ethiopia	2,000	Sudan	20,000	Saudi Arabia	60,000
Netherlands	2,000	Ghana	17,000	Ghana	50,000
Pakistan	2,000	Benin	15,000	Kazakhstan	50,000
Russia	2,000	Kazakhstan	15,000	Bulgaria	45,000
Sudan	2,000	United Kingdom	14,000	Canada	43,000
Canada	1,500	Australia	11,000	Benin	43,000
India	1,500	France	10,000	India	40,000
South Africa	1,500	Ethiopia	10,000	Uganda	35,000

Pooling BMBs into regional groupings, here is what we see:

Asia	6,968,500
Africa	2,161,000
North America	493,000
Arab World	483,500
Europe	147,800
Pacific	21,500
Latin America	8,800

I repeat: These are our brothers and sisters in the Lord, with gifts to contribute to the Body of Christ.

Specifically for the United States, here are the realities:

- The United States and Canada are the preferred destinations for harassed BMBs.

- These Christians are almost all Protestants (and in fact, almost all Evangelicals):

  ○ *Arabs:* Of the 5 million Arabs in the United States, two-thirds have a Christian background, and another 180,000 have converted from a Muslim background. These come especially from Egypt and Palestine, but increasingly there are more from Saudi Arabia, Iraq, and Syria.

  ○ *Iranians:* There are about 130,000 BMBs in the United States, part of 180,000 in the West and Middle East—plus another 500,000 or so in Iran itself. The worldwide Iranian diaspora could hold as many as 1 to 2 million BMBs.

  ○ *Other Muslim peoples* in the United States: Another 67,000 BMBs.

- Catholics in the United States: We can make only a rough estimate of 60,000 BMBs.

- Orthodox in the United States: Again, we estimate 40,000 BMBs.

Thus, the grand total for the United States is 477,000 BMBs, plus or minus 100,000. This figure has been tested through both the Operation World database and the World Christian Encyclopedia's ethno-linguistic people groups of those with a majority of Muslims in the country.

We simply must open our eyes to the values that immigrants bring to our faith. We need to remind ourselves that when Jesus healed the ten lepers, the one in whose heart a wellspring of gratitude rose up was . . . the Samaritan. The Master understandably asked, "Were not all ten cleansed? Where are the other nine? Has no one returned to give praise to God except this foreigner?" (Luke 17:17-18).

Foreigners and immigrants in our day can remind the rest of us to give praise to the God who so loved the entire world, and still does. In so doing, they bring wonderful freshness and energy to our faith.

ASK YOURSELF

- *Do you know any immigrants who are now doing well and contributing to the new setting? If so, in what ways?*
- *Do you know any immigrants who are enriching the life of the church? In what ways?*
- *Are there any immigrant congregations meeting in your local area? Have you and your congregation done anything to reach out to them in fellowship?*
- *How would your region be affected if all first-generation immigrants were to vanish?*

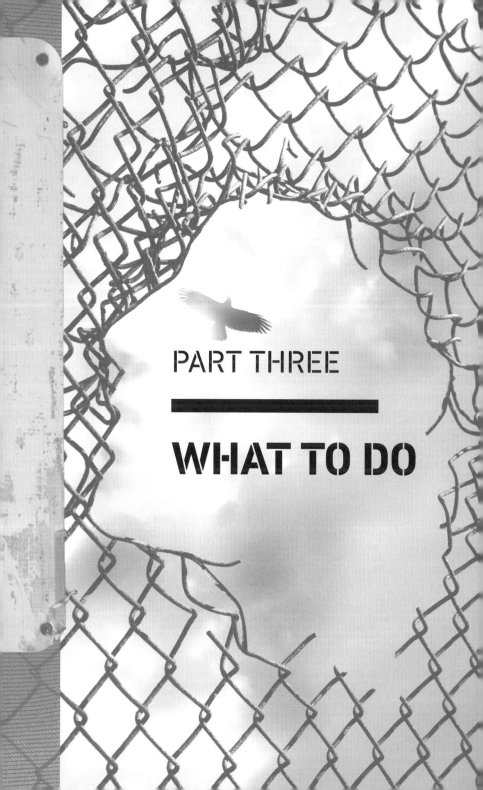

PART THREE

WHAT TO DO

CHAPTER 8

WHERE TO START

We've covered a lot of ground, reviewed numerous statistics and trends, and heard from leaders and organizations actively involved in ministering to refugees. So what do we do next? How do we begin to frame our response? Some say, "Don't begin at all—at least not yet. Let the governments tighten up their screening systems first. They need to *make sure* no terrorists are hiding among the refugees." Even a fair number of churchgoers nod in agreement.

On its December 12, 2015, cover, *The Economist* featured a pen-and-ink drawing of three prominent politicians—one American, one French, one Hungarian—under the clever headline "Playing with fear."

Others say, no, this leaves out the calling—even the risk—that is inherent in Christ's commission. "We need not choose between accepting all refugees or no refugees," writes Trevin Wax of the Gospel Project.[47] He quotes Russell Moore, president of the Ethics and Religious Liberty Commission (Southern Baptist Convention):

> The screening of refugees is a crucial aspect of national security, and we should insist on it. At the same time, evangelicals should be the ones calling the rest of the world to remember human dignity and the image of God, especially for those fleeing murderous Islamic radical jihadists. . . .

What we cannot do is to demagogue the issue, as many politicians are doing right now. An entire generation of those fleeing genocide will be asking, is there an alternative to the toxic religion they've seen. Will they hear evangelicals saying "Jesus loves you" or [arguing about] "Who then is my neighbor?" There are massive implications for both answers.[48]

It was especially ironic that just as one United States congressman was asking Secretary of State John Kerry to block refugees from settling in his district, the evangelical church he attends was exploring how to help resettle them.

Perhaps Thomas Albinson of the World Evangelical Alliance put it most succinctly when he wrote, "We cannot allow our societies to leave people to die in order to deter others from attempting to reach our borders."[49]

So, let us move forward. Where do we start? Let me propose a few steps we can take.

STEP ONE: APPRECIATING OUR STRATEGIC OPPORTUNITY

For the first time in human history, we have a reasonable assessment of where all the peoples of the world are, and how they are grouped. There is no longer any "terra incognito" on our maps, as in medieval times.

We now know much (thanks to the research of Wycliffe Bible Translators, the Joshua Project, and others) about the 13,000 or so ethno-linguistic people groups, as they are called—their numbers, their education levels, their religious allegiances, the availability of Bibles in their language, and so forth. (If you add in the concept of India's castes, the total rises closer to 17,000.)

I have taken this huge list and grouped them into 15 major blocs of peoples (East Asians, Pacific Islanders, Latin-Caribbeans, etc.) and sorted them further into 200 or so clusters of people groups we recognize more easily: "the Kurds," for example, or "the Somalis" or "the Hmong." Each of these groupings can have dozens of ethnic subgroups—some of which are still in their home areas, while others have migrated elsewhere. (My book *The Future of the Global Church* includes 56 pages of maps and diagrams to show all this.) Here's my point:

While mission efforts in the past have tended to focus on *countries*, our world is now globalizing so much that we need to focus more on reaching people groups (wherever they may reside).

The current refugee crisis makes this people groups approach all the more appropriate. One example shows why.

A third of Somalia's 12 million indigenous population has left their failed state for other places—Kenya and Ethiopia next door, Yemen and Saudi Arabia just across the Red Sea, and farther away to Europe and North America. (There in these new places, some of them are, in fact, using their mobile phones to send funds back electronically so the al-Shabaab terror group can buy more weapons!)

At present, we can't send Christian missionaries into Somalia; it's too dangerous. But we can reach Somalis in Minneapolis, in San Diego, in Bristol (England), and in the Netherlands.

The least evangelized countries of the world:
Those with less than 2% Evangelical AND less than 5% Christian

Country	% Evang	% Christian	Main Religion	Country	% Evang	% Christian	Main Religion
Tunisia	0.00	0.21	Muslim	Palestine	0.20	1.68	Muslim
Somalia	0.01	0.05	Muslim	Azerbaijan	0.21	4.37	Muslim
Yemen	0.01	0.08	Muslim	Niger	0.21	0.48	Muslim
Morocco	0.02	0.11	Muslim	Libya	0.30	2.56	Muslim
Turkmenistan	0.02	2.41	Muslim	Uzbekistan	0.33	1.23	Muslim
Mauritania	0.03	0.14	Muslim	Oman	0.35	2.52	Muslim
Maldives	0.03	0.12	Muslim	Jordan	0.39	2.55	Muslim
Afghanistan	0.03	0.04	Muslim	Gambia	0.40	4.35	Muslim
Iran	0.03	0.36	Muslim	Japan	0.46	1.63	Buddhist
Turkey	0.04	0.36	Muslim	Bhutan	0.48	0.67	Buddhist
Syria	0.06	4.62	Muslim	Pakistan	0.51	2.43	Muslim
Tajikistan	0.07	1.23	Muslim	Bangladesh	0.53	0.72	Muslim
Iraq	0.08	1.47	Muslim	Cambodia	0.79	1.73	Buddhist
Mayotte	0.11	3.00	Muslim	Saudi Arabia	0.82	4.83	Muslim
Senegal	0.11	4.68	Muslim	Mali	0.91	2.02	Muslim
Comoros	0.15	0.86	Muslim	Thailand	0.92	1.69	Buddhist
Algeria	0.16	0.36	Muslim	Mongolia	1.14	1.33	Buddhist
Israel	0.19	2.23	Jewish	Laos	1.55	2.41	Buddhist
Djibouti	0.19	4.19	Muslim				

Look at this list of the least evangelized countries of the world. Then think about how many former citizens of these unreached countries live in your city or on your street.

Ever since Christ issued His Great Commission, Christians have thought and acted globally. The flood of migrants coming in our direction helps us act globally in our own backyards. That's why the refugee "crisis" is not the end of the world. It's a strategic opportunity for unprecedented outreach to people who may have never heard or understood Christ's message. We need to view migrants as possible fertile soil for the gospel seed.

Immigrants are typically most open to change in the first years after their arrival in new places. In the 1980s I was moved to hear of the massive migrations of Sahel Africans to West Africa's coastal cities. In Abidjan, the capital of Cote d'Ivoire, many Muslim mosques flung their doors open as temporary accommodation for these immigrants. Within a short space of time, most who were not Muslim had converted to Islam.

Christian missionaries who may have spent years learning the language of a home area only to be expelled by a hostile regime are no longer obsolete. They can redeploy to new areas with immigrant populations and, using the same language, make an enormous impact. They already know the culture. They can pass this knowledge along to local churches that are floundering and wondering how to cope.

A LESSON FROM ALGERIA

A friend of mine, named Ali, is a Kabyle, an indigenous people group that has made its home in the Atlas Mountains of Algeria since before the time of Christ. (You might call them "Berbers" instead—but please don't; that name comes from "barbarian," originally a Latin slur.)

The Kabyle church was among the strongest of the early centuries. They resisted the pressures of Rome, and were greatly persecuted for it. The great defender of the faith Tertullian (approximately A.D. 155-240) was Kabyle; theologian Augustine of Hippo (A.D. 354-430) was half-Kabyle through his devout mother, Monica.

Eventually, Arab Muslims came and swept over the countryside, eradicating Christianity—but only after "ten wars with the Kabyle," they said. They systematically tried to destroy the Kabyle culture and religion. More recently, the Algerian government has kept up the pressure, trying to extinguish the Kabyle language.

But in the middle of the bloody Algerian Civil War ("the dirty war"), my friend, Ali, came in contact with a society of Catholic missionaries called "the White Fathers" (after the robes they wear). They impressed him to the point that later on some Protestant "tentmaker missionaries" were able to lead him to Jesus and then disciple him in the faith. He continued working as a telephone engineer, but in his off-work time, he (along with others) began sharing the gospel. The most amazing tide of conversions began to swell.

As far as we can reckon today, more than 300,000 Kabyle have come to Christ in the last 20 years! Additionally, some 30-80,000 Arabic-speakers have also become believers. It has become such a movement that, in 2013, the Algerian government overreacted, ordering that all churches not already registered would have to close. The Kabyle Christians basically refused—and have continued to carry on as before. They are too numerous for the government to control. "In almost every village and town in Kabylia now," Ali told me, "there are Christians and churches, some of them very big."

Ali's life was threatened, so he escaped to Europe as a refugee. Fortunately, the nation of France was kind enough to grant him admission. There he married a Christian woman. He now pastors a church in northern France, where he has set up a base for producing radio and TV programs (both in Kabyle and Arabic), which are beamed by satellite right across North Africa. Large numbers of people are being touched in this way.

Recently, Ali and his team held a conference in a West African city, where house church leaders from all across the Maghreb (Libya to Mauritania) came together for training and encouragement.

I tell this story to illustrate how, when Christians come under pressure and are forced to emigrate, the result can be positive. Ministry can penetrate back into the areas from which they were driven.

STEP TWO: RECOGNIZING AND ADMITTING PAST MISTAKES

Once I was speaking at a conference in southeast Nigeria. I reflected on the awful way my native England, after 160 years of colonial rule, had relinquished control at last. We basically handed over the northern belt to Muslim leaders to run as they saw fit.

These leaders imposed Islam as fast as they could, much to the dismay of the majority, which at that time were not Muslim. The unfortunate outcome continues to plague Nigeria to this day.

"I apologize for what Britain did to this country," I said.

One man burst into tears of gratitude! "I've never heard anybody from Britain say something like this," he cried. "We live with the result of errors of judgment by the colonial powers."

On other occasions I've gone on to admit that the heart of British expansion in the 1800s was to build a trading empire. The colonies' raw materials were to feed homeland industries, thus giving Britain a ready and exclusive market for finished goods across large portions of the world.

Let me cite just one example. The Indians were superb at making paper (thus the term "India paper," which is still in use today). It was all done by hand in those years. Then came Britain's machines, which undercut the Indian paper industry.

The same was true of India's wonderful cloth products—again, all produced manually. But it couldn't compete with the massive cotton mills of northern England.

Many products were, in fact, forbidden to be made in India lest they impinge on British sales.

On the political front, further apologies are due. During World War I, the dashing adventurer Lawrence of Arabia helped the Arab tribes chase out their overlords, the Turks. This saved the British army a lot of casualties. In return, the British basically promised the Arabs that after the war, they could rule themselves.

But the French wanted some ongoing control in the area, so a secret deal was made between the two European powers, the Sykes-Picot Agreement of 1916. France would get to administer Lebanon and Syria, while Britain could manage the rest. Lines were drawn on a Middle Eastern map without any understanding of the consequences—straight lines across the desert sands that still aggravate the situation today. ISIS has openly stated that one of its goals is to reverse Sykes-Picot.

My country is not the only one with apologies to make. There's a place in every society for admitting that our forefathers did wrong. We can't go back and change what happened. But repentance is in order, and it can be healing.

How much of Central America's refugee surge northward is due to the hunger for drugs in the United States? The drug gangs have taken virtual control of some countries, because there is huge money to be made. If there were no North American markets for cocaine and the other narcotics and with users willing to pay almost any price for their fixes, gangs wouldn't have a business.

If you are a poor Latino family living scared because the cartel runs your town and the police are totally intimidated, wouldn't you want to get your children out of harm's way? Lectures from Anglo politicians to "stay in your place" fall on deaf ears when the speakers don't acknowledge what the "place" is like, and why.

> There's a place in every society for admitting that our forefathers did wrong. We can't go back and change what happened. But repentance is in order, and it can be healing.

No wonder the Communists have made such headway over the years by reproaching what they call "economic imperialism," meaning that the rich manipulate supplies to their own advantage. One example is the banana industry, where many workers earn a pittance on massive plantations. Coffee-growing is another. Today, the "fair trade" concept is trying to reverse this, pressing for growers to get a higher proportion of the proceeds.

One of the best ways for a developing country to improve—and thereby reduce the outflow of refugees—is to work toward secondary industries that make use of its raw materials. If we in the West would empower others to get to the point of actually producing quality products for export, the returns would be impressive, and the social disruptions would diminish.

Do we have eyes to see? Do we have honest words to admit our complicity in the pressures that drive many refugees to desperate action? Recognizing and admitting past mistakes can help heal the wounds of the past while paving the way for future outreach.

STEP THREE: BECOME MORE SENSITIVE TO OTHER CULTURES

Most of us give lip service to the concept of cultural sensitivity. But the hard work of listening and truly understanding what different societies value sometimes gets short-circuited. In presenting the gospel, it is important to know the many layers of meaning and context.

Tass Abu Saada, a Palestinian Christian, writes in his forthcoming book, *The Mind of Terror:*

> If you live in any of the Western societies, you tend to view yourself mainly as an individual. From early years you've heard such sayings as "Stand on your own two feet" . . . "Be your own person" . . . "Never mind what others say about you" . . . "Seize your own destiny" . . . "You're the captain of your own ship."

> If family members or neighbors disapprove of something you're doing
> . . . well, that's their problem, you tell yourself. You've got to march to
> the beat of your own drummer. . . .
>
> I have an announcement for you: This isn't how the majority of
> the world operates. Certainly not the Muslim world. Yes, there
> are written laws to be followed—but deeper inside, people are not
> individualistic; they are collectivist. They see themselves as part of
> larger groupings—the family, the village, the tribe, the umma (Arabic
> for the worldwide body of Islam followers). How the group views a
> person is of utmost importance.[50]

I have known of numerous people who came out of Islam but ended up isolated and lonely, cut off from their family. They didn't get the welcome in the Christian community that they had hoped for. (Christians were too busy asking one another, "What if he's a spy?") Often these seekers have gone back to Islam.

The famous Great Commission verses (Matthew 28:19-20) have been translated poorly. Most English Bibles have a rendering similar to the Revised Standard Version's "Go and make disciples of all nations. . . ."

Almost every word and phrase has been inadequately translated, and this changes the theology and meaning! It should say, "In going, disciple (*verb*) all nations . . ." (my translation).

The fact that English does not have an official verb meaning "to disciple" forces meaning on other parts of the command. It encourages the idea of extracting converts out of nations to become disciples. What the text is actually saying is that we should affect individuals, families, and their whole societies.

I am glad to see more mission efforts concentrating on connecting with whole families. Expecting a Muslim-background child or teenager to stand openly for Christ against his or her family is highly unlikely. If a grown man becomes a believer alone, he may lose his wife and children.

But once a family gets interested in discipleship, the local neighbors and relatives find it much harder to object. Their usual pressures don't work as well.

I hear people in the West complaining about refugee groups that don't seem to assimilate into the host society. Whose fault is that? If all they have gotten upon arrival is a government roof over their heads and a monthly check, what should we expect? We cannot blame them if we've isolated them socially.

These are some of the factors that we must comprehend as we begin refugee ministry.

STEP FOUR: BELIEVE THAT GOD TRULY CARES ABOUT MIGRANTS

Our familiarity with certain Bible stories can dull us to the special concern God has always shown for the displaced.

Earlier in chapter 5, we highlighted Abram and Sarai, their grandson Jacob, his son Joseph, Ruth the Moabite, and, of course, the young Jesus with his parents fleeing to Egypt. But the full list is much longer. It includes

- Hagar and her teenage son, Ishmael, being evicted from Abraham's camp;

- Moses running for his life rather than trusting Egyptian justice;

- David on the run from King Saul;

- Elijah on the run from Queen Jezebel;

- Daniel and his three friends hauled off to Babylon;

- Ezra and Nehemiah;

- Aquila and Priscilla being driven out of Rome by Emperor Claudius;

- The aged apostle John, banished to a remote island along the Turkish coast—one of the same islands to which refugees are fleeing in our time.

In every case, God showed up to bring good out of chaos and to replace panic with his assurance that they were not abandoned. God also left no doubt, in His instructions across the breadth of Scripture, about how migrants should be treated. Listen to just a few of many directives that could be cited:

> "When a foreigner resides among you in your land, do not mistreat them. The foreigner residing among you must be treated as your native-born. Love them as yourself, for you were foreigners in Egypt. I am the LORD your God." (Leviticus 19:33-34)

> "You are to have the same law for the foreigner and the native-born. I am the LORD your God." (Leviticus 24:22)

> He defends the cause of the fatherless and the widow, and loves the foreigner residing among you, giving them food and clothing. And you are to love those who are foreigners, for you yourselves were foreigners in Egypt. (Deuteronomy 10:18-19)

> Do not take advantage of a hired worker who is poor and needy, whether that worker is a fellow Israelite or a foreigner residing in one of your towns. Pay them their wages each day before sunset, because they are poor and are counting on it. Otherwise they may cry to the Lord against you, and you will be guilty of sin. (Deuteronomy 24:14-15)

> "Cursed is anyone who withholds justice from the foreigner, the fatherless or the widow." (Deuteronomy 27:19)

> Solomon's prayer to God: "As for the foreigner who does not belong to your people Israel but has come from a distant land because of your name—for they will hear of your great name and your mighty hand and your outstretched arm—when they come and pray toward this temple, then hear from heaven, your dwelling place. Do whatever the foreigner asks of you, so that all the peoples of the earth may know your name and fear you, as do your own people Israel, and may know that this house I have built bears your Name." (1 Kings 8:41-43)

The Lord watches over the foreigner
    and sustains the fatherless and the widow,
    but he frustrates the ways of the wicked. (Psalm 146:9)

"You are to distribute this land among yourselves according to the
tribes of Israel. You are to allot it as an inheritance for yourselves and
for the foreigners residing among you and who have children. You
are to consider them as native-born Israelites; along with you they are
to be allotted an inheritance among the tribes of Israel. In whatever
tribe a foreigner resides, there you are to give them their inheritance,"
declares the Sovereign LORD. (Ezekiel 47:21-23)

The word of the LORD came again to Zechariah: "This is what the LORD
Almighty said: 'Administer true justice; show mercy and compassion to
one another. Do not oppress the widow or the fatherless, the foreigner
or the poor. Do not plot evil against each other.'" (Zechariah 7:8-10)

When Jesus told His sobering story about the coming judgment of the sheep
and the goats (Matthew 25:31-46), He emphasized compassion for the
"stranger." The New Century Version renders verse 35 even more vividly: "I
was alone and away from home, and you invited me into your house."

The writer of Hebrews was equally direct when he wrote, "Do not
forget to show hospitality to strangers, for by so doing some people have
shown hospitality to angels without knowing it" (Hebrews 13:2).

Dr. Thomas K. Johnson tells about highlighting this verse during a lecture in the Czech Republic, when "a young man in the class commented, 'We
Eastern Europeans have a hard time practicing hospitality because we are a
little xenophobic. We are afraid of foreigners, people who are not like us.'"

After listening to the lecture, a light went on in my mind; I noticed
that the New Testament Greek word for hospitality is *philoxenia*,
which sounds like the exact opposite of xenophobia. The word
xenophobia comes from the words *xeno* (stranger or foreign) and
phobia (fear); *philoxenia* comes from the words *philos* (friend)
and *xenia* (foreign). Therefore, in the Bible, hospitality means to

overcome xenophobia and treat a foreigner like a friend. This group of future church leaders recognized that to become godly leaders and practice Christian hospitality, they had to consciously overcome their xenophobia.[51]

It is safe to say that God is not all that interested in our xenophobia, no matter how deeply ingrained it may be. He calls us throughout Scripture to the exact reverse.

STEP FIVE: START PRAYING!

As we face the massive changes that the refugee situation brings into our areas as well as the discomfort that arises, we can stabilize our minds and hearts by seeking the face of our heavenly Father. Only from Him can we imbibe His perspective on this very emotional subject.

A number of organizations have emerged to encourage prayer:

- "Thirty Days of Prayer for the Muslim World" (during Ramadan) is one of these (see www.30daysprayer.com).

- The Fellowship of Faith for Muslims is another (see www.ffm.org.uk or www.ffmna.org).

Some of these ministries are truly global; in fact, on other continents I see a far greater dedication to prayer for the nations than I see in the West. Perhaps we are too wrapped up in technology and church growth theories to engage in much down-on-our-knees prayer. Our countries are importing immigrants, but we're not praying enough.

J. Kwabena Asamoah-Gyadu, an esteemed Ghanaian professor who has taught at Harvard as well as several United States seminaries, has written:

> I have sat through African immigrant revival meetings in Amsterdam, Hamburg, Columbus (Ohio), and Chicago in which intense prayers have been uttered for the Lord to open the eyes of the West that it may return to him as Lord. 'The battle is spiritual,' one prayer leader proclaimed, and 'we must fight it in the power of the Spirit.'[52]

After all, many refugees themselves have learned firsthand the value of prayer. Dr. Asamoah-Gyadu tells:

> It is not uncommon for prayer centers in Ghana and Nigeria to receive potential migrants, who come with their passports for prayer and anointing as they apply for visas or, if already secured, for protection and success on the journey. . . . Faith and spirituality are important in the lives of these migrants and they carry those with them everywhere.[53]

I have seen, across my half-century of ministry, the power of prayer to advance God's purposes in the world. In fact, when I look back I see a pattern. . . .

The *1960s* were *Africa's* breakthrough time. Independence was coming, which gave rise to indigenous churches that no longer had to answer to Western masters. There was a very strong focus on prayer.

In the *1970s, Latin America* seemed to come to the forefront. There was an amazing move of nominal Catholics becoming alive in a biblical faith. Brazilian churches in particular began having all-night prayer meetings on Friday nights.

I have seen, across my half-century of ministry, the power of prayer to advance God's purposes in the world.

The spotlight of the *1980s* was more on *East Asia*. A great breakthrough for the gospel came in China. The "Cultural Revolution" had collapsed (1976), and house churches began to grow. We reckon today that China has more than 100 million Christians, nearly all with strong loyalties to the Scriptures. The nation is rapidly becoming one of the most Christian nations on earth—in answer to prayer. And wherever you go among the Chinese diaspora today (Singapore, as just one example), you find large, mature churches.

The *1990s* brought the breakthrough in the Communist world. The Ukrainians became great missionaries to the rest of the formerly Soviet regions, at least for a time.

In the *2000s*, it seemed that Muslims started coming to Christ in large numbers.

And so I say, the flow of current refugees is partly an answer to prayer. These are people who need the gospel, and then they will take the gospel onward. As excited as we might be about the impact of prayer in past decades, let us be even more energized to pray for God to mold the countries of the future—including our own.

ASK YOURSELF

- *Up to this point, have you tended to view immigration as more of a headache or a spiritual opportunity? How are you modifying your perspective?*
- *How far should we apologize for mistakes of the past (slavery, colonial rule, war, exploitation)? Do you think apologizing would do anyone any good, or just pick old scabs?*
- *Which cultures do you personally find it easiest to get to know?*
- *When immigrants come, how much adapting should they do, and how much should we do?*
- *In what ways can we help new arrivals adapt to their surroundings?*

CHAPTER 9

ACTION LEVEL ONE: WHAT INDIVIDUALS CAN DO

In the Introduction, I wrote about our natural tendency to view immigrants as "those people"—a group unlike ourselves. I pointed out that many of our ancestors were migrants themselves in an earlier time.

A parallel thought-pattern emerges now that we are considering what should be done in response to the migrant crisis.

"Well, the government needs to do such-and-such," many people say.

"The United Nations should take action. . . ."

"The churches need to get together and organize a strategic plan. . . ."

"Mission agencies should mobilize their people to   "

We conveniently excuse ourselves as individuals. But should we?

OPEN HEARTS

When ordinary Christians move out of their comfort zones and casually come alongside someone from another culture, it often leads to a friendship. Making the effort to contact people on a train or in the marketplace can lead to remarkable outcomes. Some of these people are, in fact, very lonely. They silently wonder if anyone would want to get to know them.

That is what the New Testament writer meant by directing us to show simple hospitality to strangers (Hebrews 13:2). The righteous man, Job, was able to say that "No stranger had to spend the night in the street, for my door was always open to the traveler" (Job 31:32).

Tass Saada's book has an entire chapter entitled, "What You Can Do to Neutralize Terrorism." He says:

> Nothing good is going to happen as long as you hold Muslims at arm's length. Somebody has to break the ice. And it might as well be you. One of the great lines from Desmond Tutu, noted South African archbishop and Nobel laureate, is this: "If you want peace, you don't talk to your friends. You talk to your enemies."
>
> When you see a covered woman in the checkout line, go ahead and strike up a conversation. "It's a hot day today, isn't it?" . . . "Look at this bargain I found!" . . . "How old is your baby? She's adorable" . . . "What's her name?" When the mom answers, you'll be in a perfect position to follow up with "Is that an Arabic name? What does it mean?" If you hear any kind of accent, you can say, "Were you born in this country, or have you come from somewhere else?" Soon the dialogue is off and running. You're well on your way to making a new friend.[54]

(Many more helpful tips come in the rest of Saada's chapter—do's and don'ts, what foods to share, and how to open up the spiritual dimension over time.)

A pastor named Tyler Johnson in Phoenix, Arizona—just 200 miles from the Mexican border and home to hundreds of thousands of undocumented Hispanic immigrants—says, "People will argue about politics, but you can't argue with experience. When [our members] get to know an immigrant, the change we see is astounding. Eventually they begin asking, 'What can we do to address this problem in the community?'"[55]

Not everyone in Phoenix is this openhearted, however. Gary Kinnaman, former pastor of a megachurch there, told *Christianity Today*, "When it comes to immigration, some people in our churches spend more time listening to talk radio or television than the Word of God. If a pastor even broaches the issue of immigration, there is often a firestorm of opposition." He speaks from experience.[56]

But if we talk to individual refugees, asking questions, listening to their stories, hearing the agonies they have endured, and understanding why they felt they had to leave, our hearts will soften.

INTRODUCING THE GREAT PHYSICIAN

A great example of inviting Christ into the immediate problems of refugees is this report from Lebanon, a country awash in displaced people from neighboring countries:

> While Syrian and Iraqi refugees may face prejudice and social difficulties in Middle Eastern countries accepting them—Jordan, Lebanon, and Turkey—Christians are opening their arms to them. In Lebanon, an indigenous ministry leader opens church doors on Friday evenings to refugee families for coffee, socializing, and sharing about Jesus.
>
> "We often see miraculous answers to prayer," he said, adding that one of his team members had been meeting for Bible study with a Muslim woman named Yana, who was beginning to believe the Bible was God's truth.
>
> "Her brother was very ill and was told by a doctor that he had to be hospitalized immediately or he would die," he said. "Having no money, Yana pleaded for prayer for her brother. Soon after being prayed for, the brother's fever left, and he stopped coughing up blood."
>
> Yana rushed to the doctor to tell him her brother no longer needed hospital treatment, but the doctor didn't believe her.
>
> "Together they went to the home of Yana's brother, and the doctor was able to see for himself that the illness was completely gone," the ministry director said. "The doctor was completely amazed and described it as a miracle. Yana accepted the Lord Jesus into her life and went on to share the good news with all her neighbors."
>
> As a result, at least 15 of the neighborhood women have approached the ministry team, asking for prayer and visits to their home, and they also have been declaring the power of prayer in Christ's name.[57]

THE KIND ESCORT

A similar heart of outreach and compassion shows through when you talk to an ordinary Miami woman named Martha Gonzalez. She's a volunteer with a Christian ministry that receives UACs (Unaccompanied Alien Children) picked up by the United States Border Patrol and works to place them with relatives or friends already living in the States.

When, after several weeks, these frightened, even traumatized boys or girls are ready to fly from Miami to some other strange city where their relative will receive them, Gonzalez serves as their warm, trustworthy, Spanish-speaking escort.

"I'm supposed to be retired!" she says with a laugh. "But these are humble, poor kids with a good heart. Most of them have left their countries because of hunger, or being pushed into gangs. Even worse, some of them have been trafficked. Their families have gotten concerned and have arranged to send them to *El Norte*."

One boy, 13 or 14 years old, told Gonzalez on the plane ride about growing up with his grandfather in a Central American country. The old gentleman would read to him, and tell him family stories. "I could tell he had been raised well up to this point," Gonzalez says. "He talked about wanting to go to school. Now he would be going to meet his father, who had left for the United States when he was young. I just listened to the boy's dreams and assured him he could be successful in this country."

On another flight with two Honduran boys, the escort found an opening to talk about the Shepherd of lost souls, Jesus. By the time the plane landed, both boys had invited Christ into their lives. Upon landing, she walked with them outside the terminal to meet their father and even to have lunch together before she would fly back to Miami.

As the meal was served, she said to the older boy, "Tell your dad what happened to you today."

"I accepted the Lord today," he quietly replied.

The father started weeping. He said he had tried to teach his sons about spiritual things in the past, and they had mostly ignored his words. But now, everything would be different.

Gonzalez's heart for this ministry is partly founded in being an immigrant herself. Her family escaped communist Cuba in a fishing boat under cover of night when she was just 14. "I remember how traumatic it was for me," she says. "I didn't know the language. I had left behind half of my relatives and all my friends. So I can identify with these kids' fears."

Now whenever she conveys a young person to their relative in the United States, she has two parting words of advice. "Number 1—don't forget to thank God that you actually made it here! Some don't get this far. And Number 2—make sure you be thankful to this country and give back what you can in a good way. That means staying out of trouble, going to school, and making a contribution here." The wide-eyed kids nod their heads in agreement before this wise *abuela* (grandmother) who has shown the love of Christ to them.

DO THE OBVIOUS

Not everyone has access to do what Martha Gonzalez does, but everyone can look for openings. Often they are right in front of us, without the need for a lot of maneuvering. When a crowd, convicted by the preaching of John the Baptist, asked, "'What should we do then?' . . . John answered, 'Anyone who has two shirts should share with the one who has none, and anyone who has food should do the same'" (Luke 3:10-11). In other words, don't overthink this; do the obvious!

The tax collectors came up next, and got the same treatment: "Don't collect any more than you are required to" (v. 13). Soldiers were told to stop extorting money and accusing people falsely; instead, "be content with your wages" (v. 14). Nothing complicated here; instead, practical steps of honesty and compassion.

In the midst of a refugee crisis, Christian individuals must not shrink back at the complexity of the issue. Too many anxious people are waiting and hoping for some kind of help—today.

ASK YOURSELF

- *Would you be willing to welcome an immigrant into your home for an evening? Have you ever tried?*
- *Do you ever pray for your immigrant neighbors?*
- *When an immigrant is maligned, joked about, or taken advantage of, have you ever risen to their defense?*

CHAPTER 10

ACTION LEVEL TWO: WHAT LOCAL CHURCHES CAN DO

Where will I fit in?, the refugee silently wonders.
What group will accept me?
Who will show kindness to my children?
Where do I belong in this new place?

The obvious answer to these questions—at least in the mind of God—is the local church. Clearly, the church is visible, tangible, and nearby. It is the natural solution for the fears and apprehensions that beset immigrant minds.

Pastor Tony Acheampong, a Ghanaian who leads an international church in Denmark, says that, regarding many people on the move, "Before they are [even] given their boarding passes and take their seats in the plane, they are looking for a church. It is like there is something inside of them waiting for something to happen."[58]

In this chapter, we will explore many ways a local body of Christ can connect with new arrivals in helpful, nonthreatening ways. But first, we must deal with a lurking question in many congregations.

DO WE ACTUALLY *WANT* TO WELCOME
THESE PEOPLE?

If pastors and lay leaders sense hesitation or opposition among their members, even unspoken, this reluctance to help must be addressed and defused. Before programs are set up, the hidden feelings we explored back in chapter two need attention that is loving but also biblical.

One place to start is to put onto the church calendar World Refugee Sunday, which comes every year in June. Many resources are available (in six languages), from videos and maps to Scripture readings and even sermon outlines; see www.refugeehighway.net/resources/world-refugee-sunday.

There's also a nine-session curriculum for classes and small groups called, "Welcoming the Stranger: Discovering and Living God's Heart for Immigrants" (http://welcomingthestranger.com/sites/default/files/page/files/Welcoming_the_Stranger_Learning_Group_Ed2_0.pdf). It unfolds Scripture and our mission in the context of today's realities.

If church leaders feel inadequate to advance this topic, they can invite outside experts to come in and do training. Mission agencies (both denominational and independent) will be able to provide instruction on how to relate to Muslims, for example, or how to understand cross-cultural dynamics. Unfortunately, even the basic seminary training today is often weak on equipping pastors for a multicultural world (unless they are majoring in "missions"). It's simply not in the core of most seminaries' curriculum, but this gap must be filled.

Pastors who are willing may peruse the preaching helps at the Evangelical Immigration Table website (www.EvangelicalImmigrationTable .com/Preach), which offers not only sermon suggestions but videos of actual messages given by a wide variety of speakers.

This kind of groundwork is necessary in order to exhibit a genuinely welcoming attitude. Otherwise, immigrants will be able to "smell" that they are being only tolerated, not wanted.

Dr. Bradley Wright, a sociologist at the University of Connecticut, ran an intriguing test by sending inquiry emails to 3,120 randomly selected

United States churches, from Baptist to Lutheran, Catholic to Pentecostal, pretending to be a family moving into the local area and wanting information about service times, size of the congregation, youth programs, and so forth.

The trick was in how the emails were signed. "Greg Murphy" and "Scott Taylor" represented white inquirers. "Jamaal Washington" and "Tyrone Jefferson" represented blacks. "Carlos Garcia" and "Jose Hernandez" represented Hispanics. "Wen Lang Li" and "Jong Soo Kim" represented Asian-Americans.

Which names would get prompt responses, and at what length? Which would be ignored?

> For every 100 churches that replied to . . . a white-sounding name, 93 replied to those with black- or Hispanic-sounding names, and 85 to Asian-sounding names. . . . Think about it. A letter simply having the "wrong" name significantly reduced these churches' likelihood of welcoming a potential visitor.[59]

Refugees and other immigrants are most often *not* going to fit the prevailing mode in a congregation. They will be "the other." Are we all right with that? Do we actually want to welcome them?

If so, then we are ready to proceed with action on their behalf.

EIGHT WAYS TO REACH OUT AND TOUCH IMMIGRANTS

Here are some options (certainly not all) for connecting with new arrivals. (It goes without saying that all of these options need to be offered *free,* since the people we seek to touch have minimal funds).

1) Language classes/tutoring. If migrants need to make a change from their mother tongue, this need is obvious. The quicker they can grasp basic English (or German, Swedish, Dutch, whatever), the sooner they will be able to find employment and navigate the many other challenges of daily life.

To gain citizenship, knowledge of the local language is almost mandatory. The United States, for example, requires all applicants to pass an English examination (unless the person is elderly and has already lived in the country for 15 or more years).

2) Mother-and-toddler groups. All across the globe, mothers with little ones naturally gravitate to each other. What better way to pull an immigrant woman out of the shadows than by offering a warm and inviting place for her to socialize with others at her station of life?

3) Job guidance. Helping the new arrival through the maze of employment listings, workforce centers, and online opportunities can be a huge help. Young women who arrive hoping to find work as au pairs/nannies need assistance in knowing where to look—and how not to be taken advantage of.

Some migrants arrive with professional qualifications—nurses, teachers, lab technicians, to name just a few—but they must prove their credentials to new (and often skeptical) gatekeepers. Otherwise, they will not be allowed to use their talents in the new place. What a relief to have a church friend alongside them during this challenging process. If further education is required, the local friend can point out where to get it and how much it will cost.

In addition, some church members who own businesses or have hiring authority in their companies may be positioned to offer employment directly to the new arrivals. This gives them the added blessing of working for a Christian boss.

4) Sports teams and leagues. Any activity that involves a ball will quickly serve as a magnet for migrant young people. They don't need to know the language so long as they can get onto a field, pitch, or court with others their age. Within minutes they feel welcomed.

5) Legal guidance. This is a paramount need for refugees, obviously. And the field can be even more confusing and obtuse than searching for a job. It is hardly fair for any Christian to complain about undocumented immigrants if we are not willing to help them sort out their cases, find the proper government paperwork, fill it out correctly, and get the documents they need.

Several denominations and groups in the United States have banded together to form The Immigration Alliance, equipping local churches to provide fair, trustworthy counsel on everything from applying for legal status to determining eligibility for health benefits to dealing with the police if victimized by crime. The Alliance provides rigorous training so that local-church volunteer paralegals know what they're talking about and can guide clients suitably. For more information, go to: www.theimmigrationalliance.org.

Meanwhile in the UK, Churches Together in Britain and Ireland (CTBI) have stimulated much activity in negotiating with governments and encouraging city-wide initiatives to welcome refugees. To learn more, see: https://ctbi.org.uk/how-the-churches-are-responding-to-the-refugee-crisis.

6) Temporary housing. When Pope Francis called for every Catholic parish to take in a refugee family—starting at the Vatican itself—I thought it was a courageous challenge. Many Protestant congregations have done this as well. In fact, every congregation should ask itself, "What about us?"

Space may be available in some church buildings themselves. If not, what else is nearby at an affordable cost? The point here is not to provide permanent residence; it is rather to simply offer shelter in the current moment of need.

7) Special holiday events. Churches can invite immigrants to parties that celebrate, for example, New Year's Day, Thanksgiving, or the national holiday, with games for the children and simple explanations for the adults on why this day is meaningful in the culture.

8) Social invitations to homes. Immigrants naturally wonder how we actually live day to day. Nothing quite says welcome like being invited to the home of a Christian. It speaks volumes about openheartedness and good will. The conversation that flows in an evening spent together around a table can pay immeasurable benefits.

International students especially crave this kind of welcome. Yet, according to one study, 80 percent of these who graduate from United States colleges have never been inside an American home.

Those who do get invited for true Christian hospitality can find it to be life-changing, or at least assumption-changing. Even if they do not convert to our faith, they go away with a positive impression.

BOXES OF LOVE

If you were to spend much time around 600-member Community Church Derby in the UK East Midlands, you would see and hear many of these activities running at full speed. It was not always so; as recently as 2011 the congregation was only around 3 percent of foreign origin. Today, that figure is 20 percent, the majority being of Muslim background. In fact, the church just baptized its forty-ninth Iranian member!

A fair amount of leadership for this has come from Adam and Karina Martin. They joined the pastoral team after years of working in Estonia, bringing with them a heart for cross-cultural outreach. One of the most novel ideas is taking "Welcome Boxes" to new arrivals—a brightly wrapped shoebox filled with small gifts. Delivered with a smile, these presents say that the immigrants and their children are valued and cared for. More than one astonished refugee parent has said, "You are the first person we've met who wasn't a government official!"

Started first at Christmastime, the Welcome Box outreach has grown into a year-round ministry, with many volunteers involved in providing, packing, and distributing. Once inside the home or apartment, questions about the church's other services to immigrants naturally flow.

Other churches around the UK are picking up on this idea and developing their own programs. (For more information, see www.welcomechurches.org.)

A related effort, also based on the Community Church site, is the Mahabba Network, which seeks to motivate and mobilize everyday Christians to love their Muslim neighbors as well as help churches to mentor and multiply communities of disciples. (Mahabba is the Arabic word for "love" or "affection.") It has some 40 prayer groups around the country and beyond, which naturally express their hearts through local projects and outreaches. (For details see http://www.mahabbanetwork.com.)

ALWAYS SEEK TO "NETWORK" FOR CHRIST

Whether the topic is language acquisition, job hunting, legal procedures, or anything else, the local church should always be looking for ways to invite the Friend of Immigrants into the conversation. There's no need to avoid mentioning Christ. Government agencies may be constrained by "politically correct" rules and policies, but the local church is free to speak its truth.

In fact, the immigrant will think it odd if you *don't* introduce your faith and the efficacy of prayer to a God who hears and responds. They will wonder if you are ashamed of your beliefs for some reason.

In a neighborhood of Berlin, Pastor Gottfried Martens regularly baptizes Iranian and Afghan asylum seekers who have been touched by Trinity Church's message and welcome. Attendance at this Evangelical congregation has swelled from 150 to more than 600 in just two years—in Germany, no less, where many other churches struggle. The newcomers, having received help with their legal applications, readily sign up for Martens's three-month "crash course" in Christianity.

> **Immigrants will think it odd if you *don't* introduce your faith. They will wonder if you are ashamed of your beliefs for some reason.**

"I know there are people coming here because they have some kind of hope regarding their asylum," the pastor acknowledges. "But I am inviting them to join because I know that whoever comes here will not be left unchanged."

One carpenter, Mohammed Ali Zonoobi, said he had attended secret meetings back in Iran ever since friends gave him a Bible at age 18. Now with a wife and two children, he had decided to flee to Germany after several Christian friends were arrested for practicing their faith.

"Now we are free and can be ourselves," says his wife, Afsaneh (who since her baptism has chosen the name "Katarina" instead). "Most important, I am so happy that our children will have a good future here." For this family, the light of a gospel-sharing church has changed everything.[60]

STRUCTURAL ADJUSTMENTS

This kind of happy result will, over time, require change. As more and more immigrants come into the pews, many may wonder if they are also welcome on the boards and committees of a congregation, or among the leadership.

Kensington Baptist Church in Bristol, the U.K.'s eighth largest city, used to be all Caucasian in a genteel Victorian neighborhood of four-story houses. But their vision for reaching other ethnicities has borne much fruit in recent years, to the point that they have added a South Asian pastor to their team.

In this way, they are looking more like the leadership of the first-century Antioch church, which included a Jew from Cyprus (Barnabas), two North Africans (Simeon and Lucius), a former Pharisee (Saul/Paul), and the politically connected "Manaen (who had been brought up with Herod the tetrarch)" (Acts 13:2). No wonder this church became the beating heart of missionary endeavors throughout the entire eastern Roman empire, with an obvious concern for all people groups.

In some cases, as numbers increase in an indigenous church, it may be wise to sponsor an ethnic congregation (or at least a Bible study), making use of the facility for services at a different time of the week. But some factors call for closer examination. The host church should not be content just to be a "landlord," renting out its space. The truth is, any diaspora church has only a lifespan of about one-and-a-half generations. I see this everywhere, whether observing Afro-Caribbean churches in my home country, Korean or Chinese churches in North America, or BMB (believers-with-a-Muslim-background) churches across Europe.

Why is that, you ask? While the first generation relishes the familiarity of their home language and culture, their children want to assimilate into the new environment. They don't want to keep being "immigrant kids." They want to speak, dress, and act like their peers in school and the community. As soon as they are old enough to make their own choices, they will merge into the mainstream.

So what is the answer? It is for pastors and boards—indigenous and ethnic—to build a long-term future together, by praying and planning together. While the ethnic worship service can continue for a season, the young people must be welcomed into the indigenous youth programs.

"There is a Danish church," Hans-Henrik Lund reports from Copenhagen, "which hosts a Vietnamese church and Burmese church, but the children all go to Sunday school together, while the Vietnamese and Danish churches have their [adult] services. The Sunday school is 100 percent Danish, but the children are from all the different cultures. Then they eat together, and the Burmese church has their services in the afternoon."

Lund, who heads up the national Kirkenes Integrations Tjeneste ("Churches Integration Service"; see www.kit-danmark.dk), says, "We encourage the Danish churches to . . . have cooperation—maybe meet together two or three times a year, have a common service where you do it in Danish and another language. Also, [we recommend that they] make social arrangements—for example, meet on a Saturday to clean the church, or go to the park and have a picnic together."[61]

The two populations (made up of teens but also adults) can plan and engage in outreach ministry together, showing the world a powerful witness of "one body" in Christ. Perhaps in the future, multicultural teams can even be sent on short-term mission trips to refugee camps abroad.

COMPLICATIONS? OF COURSE!

Are there difficulties to work out along the way? Certainly. Understanding the subtle difference between cultures does not come naturally to any of us.

Some ethnic groups are glad to hug one another, while others find this too familiar. Some cultures do not even shake hands—certainly not between a man and a woman. We won't know these things until we pay attention, perhaps even asking for guidance: "Tell me how you do this in your culture; I'd really like to know."

One multiethnic church in Columbus, Ohio (United States), found that when white members addressed the pastor by his first name, black members found this disrespectful; it should be "Pastor Johnson," not "Mike" or "Jim."[62]

Again, Hans-Henrik Lund tells: "Danish people are very clear on rules, and there can be a lack of flexibility. So a migrant church could be thrown out if their service is too loud, or they don't have the same expectations of cleanliness, or the rent isn't paid on the first of the month."

Nearby Pastor Tony Acheampong adds, "We must be able to accommodate each other and meet halfway somewhere."[63]

Sharing food can be a wonderful way to bond—or not. James Watson, a consultant for the Salvation Army in Canada and Bermuda, explains how this can be managed.

> . . . a very memorable 'pot luck' luncheon at the House of Prayer for All Nations. The church planters had effectively built relationships with their neighbors, and about half the people who arrived through the long morning worship service (or perhaps just for the pot luck at the end) were newcomers to Canada. We were blessed at these

worship services to have neighbors encounter the gospel for the very
first time.

> [But] we had to label the three different tables for the buffet: "vege-
> tarian" (for friends from Hindu regions), "halal" (for friends from
> Islamic countries) and "we don't know what's in it" (the eat-at-your-
> own-risk table). The wide range of food options reflected the diversity
> of conversations as people ate together.[64]

Perhaps the trickiest is the area of finances. Indeed, it is a blessing to give
to migrants and migrant communities in need—but it can also be a danger, if it continues to the point of breeding dependency. It is hard to say
how much is too much.

Say a church has rooms that can be used by a refugee family. That is
fine—but if nothing further is done to teach them the local language, to
help them find some kind of job, and to equip them for moving into some
kind of permanent housing, we have done them no favors.

If you or I were standing along the road as Syrian refugees came stum-
bling along in the heat, of course we would give out bottles of water. But
over time, we want our gifts to enable ongoing stability rather than just
survival. We don't want our support to lead to permanent reliance.

However . . . if we are not careful, this thinking can lead to an excuse
for doing nothing: *My grandfather came to this country and worked in the
coal mines, pulling himself up by his bootstraps. These people need to do the
same.* Such hardheartedness is not pleasing to God.

CHANGE IS PART OF THE PACKAGE

All that we have been describing adds up to the necessity for change—
which is not something every church is good at doing. But the fact
remains that when countries and cities and neighborhoods change, the
indigenous church has to adapt—or relocate—or else die. Our world is
becoming more and more multicultural every day.

For people of varying backgrounds and church traditions, change can be hard. But if we pray together, we often find a transcending friendship that allows for change.

I will go so far as to say that *any congregation not yet reflecting the ethnic ratios within walking distance of its building has not yet adapted enough.* Perhaps you will disagree, calling this benchmark too high. I do not.

It is so easy for us as private citizens to expect that government placement agencies will teach newcomers how to get along in a new culture. Maybe they will, but maybe not. In all too many places, Christian bodies have to pick up the slack. A lot of good things are just not going to happen if local churches don't do them.

Our God cast His vision long ago through the prophet Isaiah:

Let no foreigner who is bound to the Lord say,
   "The LORD will surely exclude me from his people.". . .
For this is what the LORD says . . .

"Foreigners who bind themselves to the Lord
   to minister to him,
to love the name of the LORD,
   and to be his servants,
all who keep the Sabbath without desecrating it
   and who hold fast to my covenant—
these I will bring to my holy mountain
   and give them joy in my house of prayer.
Their burnt offerings and sacrifices
   will be accepted on my altar;
for my house will be called
   a house of prayer for all nations." (Isaiah 56:3-4, 6-7)

If this was His calling under the Old Covenant, how much more under the New?

ASK YOURSELF

- *What is the present ethnic mix of your congregation? How does this align with your neighborhood?*
- *Are adjustments in your ministry programs called for? What about leadership assignments?*
- *Do any of your programs specifically address the felt needs of local immigrants?*
- *If immigrants became more visible in your church, would anyone be upset?*
- *Has your church invited those with special knowledge about immigration to come and help educate the membership? Do you know (or support) any cross-cultural mission works? How might they help you in outreach?*
- *In what way might your church help to start or strengthen a group of immigrant believers?*
- *How much of your church's missions giving is targeted to cross-cultural needs?*

CHAPTER 11

ACTION LEVEL THREE: WHAT CHRISTIAN AGENCIES CAN DO

When the apostle Paul and his associates stopped overnight at the port of Mitylene on their way to Jerusalem (Acts 20:14-15), they were on a Greek island much in our news 20 centuries later. Its name is Lesbos; in fact, Mitylene remains the capital city today. Refugees fleeing in risky boats from the nearby Turkish shore see the lights of Mitylene on the horizon.

And when (or *if?*) they make it safely ashore, followers of Paul's gospel are there to meet them. A student worker sent by the Pentecostal Assemblies of Canada (PAOC) tells about giving a blanket and some food to a drenched man "in the name of Isa al-Masih" (Jesus the Messiah).

"Who is this Isa?!" the man immediately asked in English, falling to his knees. "I want to know more about Him, because when I arrived in Turkey, He was the one who gave me food, blankets, and shelter. And now here—He is the one who gives me another blanket. He has cared for me ever since I left Syria!" At that, the man began to weep.

The student was prepared with a simple answer as well as a further gift: a Bible. The refugee thanked him profusely.

Other PAOC workers on Lesbos Island tell similar stories. Three of them, upon approaching a group of men, struck up a conversation. They mentioned that they followed Isa al-Masih and had come to this place because of His love. "Yes, we know Christians," the Syrian men replied. "And we know that they love us. Christians were the first people we met in Turkey; they gave us food, shelter, and blankets—all in the name of Isa."

By the next week, as the weather starting turning, the Canadians were back with 65 portable fireplaces to ward off the cold.[65]

ON THE FRONT LINES

Denominations and interdenominational mission groups have been on the front lines of emergency relief work for decades. The present refugee crisis is calling for greater agency response than ever.

Often the task is complex enough—logistically, financially, and politically—that it requires expert management. Local churches in the West, as much as they would like to help, are usually out of their element in trying to act alone. They need the coordination, past experience, cultural skills, language expertise, and the wisdom of special agencies.

> Denominations and interdenominational mission groups have been on the front lines of emergency relief work for decades. The present refugee crisis is calling for greater agency response than ever.

News media may not always give them the credit they deserve, attributing relief efforts solely to governments and perhaps the Red Cross/Red Crescent. But at ground level, it is obvious that Christian compassion is active, because so many workers are Christians serving Christian agencies.

A case in point: Croatia, a small Balkan nation to which refugees began flooding as soon as Hungary closed its border on September 15, 2015. Suddenly small border towns were receiving as many as 8,000 a night. Quickly, a Christian aid organization named Remar sprang into action, distributing supplies and filling up its rehabilitation house with people.

Right alongside them were workers from Cru (formerly Campus Crusade for Christ), Nazarene Compassionate Ministries (NCM), and a Samaritan's Purse Disaster Assistance Response Team. "God has given us an amazing opportunity," said Teanna Sunberg, NCM communications coordinator for Central Europe. "He's brought the Muslim world to our doorstep."

Looking over the combined efforts, the general secretary of the Baptist Union in Croatia, Željko Mraz, said, "The response is much better than I expected, considering the small size of the evangelical community in Croatia. There are many different evangelicals from different denominations involved in helping."[66]

BEHIND THE FRONT LINES

Even before refugees decide to head for the West, their peril is not going unnoticed by Christian groups.

Barnabas Fund has been actively building a coalition called "Operation Safe Havens" specifically to help Christians who are afraid to stay in refugee camps, where they are often marginalized and discriminated against by Muslim majorities. As alternatives, the coalition is arranging shelter in schools, churches, apartments, and other large buildings, along with food and other daily essentials.

"Displaced Christians in the Middle East have lost everything, but still they hope in God," says the fund's website (https://barnabasfund .org). "The British government and other Western governments are beginning to listen and to understand that Christians must be treated as a vulnerable minority."

Many such efforts are underway in the desperate regions of our world that, for security reasons, should not be broadcast.

PROCESSING AND PLACEMENT

Once a refugee, or refugee family, is cleared for resettlement, Western governments often rely on Christian organizations to escort them toward new homes.

The United States State Department, for example, has contracted with nine national agencies to handle cases, including the Evangelical group World Relief (www.wr.org), with offices in 27 cities plus 14 other nations. They recruit local congregations to form "Good Neighbor Teams" that find and furnish modest apartments as starter homes for the new arrivals. Friendship and spiritual support are offered as well.

On the European side, numerous agencies have partnering arrangements with local churches or denominations to welcome new arrivals.

MEDIA

Providers of print, radio, television, and Internet material are all at work finding ways to serve crisis zones and new immigrants. Restrictive countries that in the past were able to ban the Bible have virtually no way to block websites such as www.biblegateway.com and www.youversion.com, each of which offers translations in dozens of languages. These are being read in private homes all over the Middle East and beyond.

Television is nearly as ubiquitous; if you look at the skylines of Cairo or Istanbul or Damascus, you see a mass of satellite dishes atop rich and poor homes alike. SAT7, the Christian network based in Beirut (www.sat7.org), is just one agency having a huge impact across the region.

Even in Iran, the Christian message is being watched. At one point, the revolutionary government had banned all dishes. But then, certain cabinet ministers found they could import them illegally for installation—and thereby put a lot of money into their pockets! So dishes began to sprout on rooftops everywhere, and ministries such Elam are stepping up to teach and encourage in Christ's name. Compared to the deadly and/ or boring programs from the government, these get a large viewership.

Printed Scripture and publications have a critical role to play as well in shaping minds. Especially with new technologies such as print-on-demand, Christian groups are printing small quantities of books and magazines affordably that were not feasible before. Every effort has a role to fulfill; after all, the competition for people's thoughts is stiff. Madrassahs in New York City are giving out free copies of the Qur'an in Spanish. How much more important is the Word of Life in whatever language a person wishes to read.

In all of this media work, there is great use for first- and especially second-generation immigrants who are believers. Their language skills and cultural knowledge are priceless.

GOVERNMENT ADVOCACY

When governments need to be challenged regarding their immigration policies, Christian agencies are the natural voices to do so. Where there is unjust legislation or prejudice, we must be ready to "speak truth to power."

In the present flood of needy refugees, World Relief has been urging the United States government to admit far more than its conventional 70,000 refugees per year. Even the recent announcements about letting in 85,000 or 100,000 are inadequate, says the organization. It is pressing to get back to the level of 1980 (during the Vietnamese "boat people" crisis), when 200,000 were admitted.

> **Where there is unjust legislation or prejudice, we must be ready to "speak truth to power."**

If an individual migrant is being unfairly refused, or being deported on dubious grounds, Christian advocacy organizations can take up the cause—and often win. Some situations remind us of what Mr. Bumble said in the Charles Dickens novel *Oliver Twist,* "If the law supposes that, the law is an ass—an idiot." Alert Christian groups can coax the government bureaucracy to face what needs to be done in such a case rather than continuing to follow dusty protocols.

EDUCATION

Finally, agencies have a key role to play in educating local churches and individuals about migrant ministry. They know the subtleties of culture; they know how to access various literature tools and media; they can give weekend seminars that are highly enlightening. They can also network one church to another if both have a common vision for ethnic outreach.

Another very special role they can play is bridging the culture gap between local indigenous churches and the growing number of immigrant church fellowships sprouting up wherever immigrants settle. This enables the two types of congregations to work together in ministry to migrants, bearing long-term fruit in integrating both new converts and second and subsequent generations into the local population.

Mission specialists can also help a church think through a long-term sending policy. One of our current shortcomings in the craze for short-term mission trips is that lay people often get very little training before they travel . . . and little to no evaluation exercise once they return. The trip was flashy . . . it was fun . . . it catered to people's love of international travel—but at the end of the day, what was accomplished for the Kingdom?

I have even seen church people have a difficult experience on a trip and come home inoculated from ever considered mission work again. If there's no guidance to process what happened, they may end up wanting nothing to do with missions forever after. Wise counsel from an agency can help church leaders set realistic goals for trips that leave the site better than it was when the group arrived, and they can also disciple the next generation of Christian workers for future fruitfulness.

But of course, this means that agencies must be willing to invest personnel and time in working with local churches. Too often missionaries look at home churches only for their funding potential; *I go there to raise money for my budget.* Instead, they must also go to advance the church's ministry potential, both locally and internationally. In this way, a genuine two-way partnership is strengthened.

The same dynamic is true for seminaries. It concerns me that men and women preparing for local church ministry receive inadequate equipping for multicultural ministry. Moreover, with the pressure to offer courses that students want, missiology is often the first to be sacrificed, or treated as optional rather than a fundamental component of every course.

As a result, we are turning out graduates ill-prepared for ministry in the 21st century. But the future is multicultural, and we ought to prepare all workers for discipling in multicultural situations. Agencies can have a vital role in partnering and providing the vision and needed training skills.

ASK YOURSELF

- *Does your denomination have a department for immigrant ministry? If so, are you taking advantage of their offerings to help and support your congregation in impacting your local immigrant population? If not, who can you approach to get help?*
- *What cross-cultural training for individuals and congregations is still lacking?*
- *What physical and financial aid is going toward refugees, and how wisely is it being used to relieve distress without creating long-term dependency?*
- *What mission agencies are you already in touch with that specialize in immigrant evangelism and discipleship? If you don't have such connections, will you try to find some?*
- *Is there potential for your ministry to local migrants, eventually, to impact their countries of origin? In what ways might this come to pass?*
- *Does your agency have a global plan (not just national) for the people groups among whom it ministers?*

CHAPTER 12

ACTION LEVEL FOUR: WHAT THE GLOBAL BODY OF CHRIST CAN DO

You may find this chapter title to be preposterous, knowing (as I fully admit) that getting all of Christendom to do any one thing in concert is practically impossible. (As one Protestant said to another, "What my denomination needs is a good, strong pope—provided I could be the pope!")

Nevertheless, I want to focus here on a few things that all of us, from all the various backgrounds and church polities, can *voluntarily* do to respond in a Christlike manner to the current migrant crisis. If the watching world began to notice our initiative in these regards, it would improve our reputation in a positive direction.

SPEAK TO OURSELVES ABOUT THE NEED AT HAND

This is what the United Nations High Commissioner for Refugees asked of us when he pleaded that we work to create "space in the hearts and minds"[67] of our people for refugees and asylum seekers. He was admitting that the UN cannot do this from on high. It must rather be addressed by voices already known, trusted, and respected. Spiritual leaders will get far more acceptance than politicians on this topic of welcoming immigrants.

And they are speaking up. Here are two examples:

A veritable who's-who of United States and Canadian evangelical leaders gathered at Wheaton College a week before Christmas 2015 to consider the issue. Their closing statement was bold, including these declarations:

> Moments like this are when Christians cannot remain silent and still. In light of this crisis, we commit ourselves and our churches to actively care for and minister to global refugees with mercy and compassion, both here and abroad, based on God's compelling concern for all people in need and especially refugees.

The group did not sidestep the hesitations that many churchgoers feel, but said:

> . . . We cannot allow voices of fear to dominate. . . . We acknowledge that there are genuine security concerns and encourage governments to be stewards of safety, but we also observe that choosing to come to North America as refugees would be among the least effective ways for those who intend to do us harm.

> So, as governments oversee matters of security, we will care for the hurting. . . .

> The refugees fleeing this violence are not our enemies; they are victims. We call for Christians to support ministries showing the love of Jesus to the most vulnerable. . . . This is what Jesus did; he came to the hurting and brought peace to those in despair.[68]

In the same vein, the European Evangelical Alliance has challenged its members in a powerfully worded document entitled "5 Reasons Followers of Christ Seek the Protection and Welfare of Refugees." It calls us all to be "humble people living lives marked by mercy, justice and hospitality."

The EEA lists five reasons Christians should help refugees, starting with three reasons we have already explored in this book:

1) Forcible Displacement in the Bible (see Chapter 5, "Jesus Was A Refugee");
2) Divine Mandates Concerning the Alien (see Chapter 8, "Where to Start");
3) Jesus' Identification with the Refugee, the Returnee and the Stranger.

The EEA statement also highlights these two reasons for Christians to be involved:

4) We Are Called to Live as Aliens. "This attitude should disarm and replace xenophobia and prejudice against refugees with respect, as their lives can help us better understand our own relationship to the world as temporary residents."
5) Forced Displacement of Christ Followers. "The first wave of Christian refugees is recorded in the Book of Acts in the New Testament. They were persecuted and uprooted specifically because of their faith in Jesus. Throughout the centuries and into the present day, followers of Jesus have experienced persecution for their faith, forcing many to flee their homelands. This predisposes followers of Jesus to care about the plight of all forcibly displaced people."[69]

SPEAK TO GOVERNMENTS ABOUT CRITICAL MIGRATION ISSUES WITH MORAL DIMENSIONS

As already mentioned in the previous chapter, government quotas are more than just numbers on a spreadsheet; they represent real people in dire straits. If the quotas are lower than they need to be, voices of Christian conscience have an obligation to speak up. The more voices coming from a diversity of denominations and groups within the Body of Christ, the greater the impact.

Politicians may be too busy (or too biased) to notice which refugees are getting helped and which are getting ignored. In my country, Christian leaders have been making the case to the British government that it must give more attention to persecuted Christians in the Middle East. (One of our newer political parties is anti-immigration entirely. And it got a surprising 15 percent of the 2015 national election.)

The Archbishop of Canterbury took his concerns directly to the Prime Minister and also made a speech in the House of Lords to say that these poor souls are not receiving the publicity they should. They're being harassed by everybody—including the Western countries.

Elizabeth Kendal, an Australian analyst and advocate for religious liberty, bluntly advises:

> Instead of taking directions from regional powers Turkey, Saudi
> Arabia, and Iran—all state sponsors of terror—the West should
> prioritize protecting minorities and working in their interests, so that
> Christians might be safe in Christianity's historic heartland. To do
> that, the West might need to swallow its pride and talk to Assad and
> to Russia. Ever since the Crimean War (in the 1850s)... the West has
> backed Muslims at the expense of persecuted Christians. Surely the
> time has come for the West to be astute, identify the real enemy and
> put an end to this ruse, for the sake of imperiled Christians.[70]

Few public officeholders are going to talk this way, for fear of being "politically incorrect." Christians with a moral compass must take up the effort.

For a truly global perspective, hear the measured words of Filipino Bishop Efraim Tendero, secretary general of the World Evangelical Alliance:

> Over the last months, we have seen governments struggling to find
> a proper response to help the huge number of people fleeing conflict
> and persecution. We have seen how certain communities are excluded
> by the aid and refugee resettlement mechanisms that the United
> Nations and some European nations have implemented. Our faith
> calls us to respond in prayer and in concrete action to help and to
> speak up as the voice of those who are not heard.

And to go even further, during the coming years and decades, let us urge governments to develop policies that make local societies more free and economically viable, so that people can stay where they are instead of fleeing. This encompasses things such as curtailing corruption, setting up fair trade agreements, and making sure our aid programs do not simply prop up the elite.

The global Body of Christ must not be a bystander while desperate people run for their lives.

"The Church is the only society that exists for the benefit of those who are not its members," said Archbishop William Temple.

How true! We have the imperative of God's command to us, the motive of God's love within us, and the Holy Spirit to empower us to make a difference in lives of these millions of refugees by pleading their cause in the courts of heaven and in the political arenas of the world. Who else has the moral and ethical basis and also the cultural and spiritual tools to welcome and integrate them into the Body of Christ?

ASK YOURSELF

- *How must Christians around the world view and respond to this refugee emergency?*
- *What kinds of political action and advocacy are needed?*
- *How can we change the attitudes of evangelical churches that have often been the most xenophobic in the current refugee crisis?*
- *How can the multitude of Christian entities work together to maximize their impact?*

FOR SUCH A TIME AS THIS

I firmly believe that for Christians today, the current migrant surge is not a *problem* but a *potentiality*.

When the apostle Paul admonished us in this regard, he did not write ". . . making the most of every opportunity, though the days are evil." He wrote, ". . . making the most of every opportunity, *because* the days are evil," (Ephesians 5:16, emphasis added). He was not intimidated in the least. He saw (from his Roman prison cell) that God was up to something in the midst of persecution and social disorder.

The more we align ourselves with what Christ wants to accomplish in this season of history, the higher numbers of displaced people who will find themselves changing not only their geography but also their eternal destiny.

A young Christian named David Crabb gives a wondrous vignette of how this can play out:

> As she was browsing the children's section of our local library last week, my wife, Stephanie, met a woman from North Africa named Fatimah. Fatimah has a gregarious personality, so they quickly struck up a conversation while our two daughters read books with Fatimah's son, Mohammed.

When Fatimah was a girl, her country endured a brutal civil war that dragged on for nearly two decades and claimed half a million lives. As a result, her family fled their home and country and came to the United States. Fatimah is a refugee.

To the average person in the library that morning, Stephanie and Fatimah couldn't have seemed more different. They had radically different upbringings, spoke different languages, and dressed and acted differently. Stephanie is an evangelical Christian. Fatimah is a Sunni Muslim.

And yet, because they share a common humanity, they are remarkably similar. They laughed as they talked about raising toddlers, swapped pregnancy and birthing stories, and shared tips on their favorite local parks and restaurants. Towards the end of their conversation, Fatimah shared that she was lonely most days. Stephanie invited her over for lunch and exchanged contact information with her.

And so, because of a bloody, senseless civil war, a Muslim from a remote village in North Africa found herself forging a new friendship with a Christian. By every account, her life seems a tragedy. She's certainly a victim of great evil. But what is equally clear, for those with eyes to see, is that God is up to something good.

David Crabb goes on to address the security concerns roiling across his nation. But then he says:

What if, while America was asking questions about safety and risk management, Christians were asking, What is God doing? What if, through the senseless evil of civil war, God was bringing unreached people groups to our cities? What if, through great tragedy, God was bringing about the triumph of the gospel?

Syria has over 20 million Muslims in 18 unreached people groups. Christian missionaries have spent years praying, strategizing, and risking everything to go to these people. Now, God is bringing them

here. After raising tens of thousands of dollars, undergoing extensive
training, leaving everything familiar, and going through the grueling
process of learning a foreign language—only then could a missionary experience the breakthrough of having the kind of conversation Stephanie and Fatimah had just casually at our local library in
Minneapolis. . . .

"Is it safe?" sounds like a question a government would ask. And
it should ask; a government should seek to protect its people. But
Christians ask, "What is God up to?"[71]

This swimming against the political tide reminds me of the great statement by British pulpiteer G. Campbell Morgan (1863-1945): "The church
did the most for the world when it was least like the world." Are we bold
enough to raise a different kind of voice in the current debates? Are we
willing to operate from a stance of faith rather than fear? Can we see that
perhaps we have been placed, like Queen Esther, at this juncture of history "for such a time as this" (Esther 4:14)?

If so, we will be prepared for the solemn verdict to be announced
one day when "the King will say to those on his right, 'Come, you
who are blessed by my Father; take your inheritance, the kingdom prepared for you since the creation of the world. For I was hungry and you
gave me something to eat, I was thirsty and you gave me something to
drink, *I was a stranger and you invited me in* . . . '" (Matthew 25:34-35,
emphasis added).

Whatever questions or hesitations we might have today will fade away
in the blazing light of God's priorities. We will know we have pleased our
Lord and Master.

And that is all that matters.

We are all strangers and pilgrims here on earth. Ahead of us awaits
the greatest and most wonderful final migration of history—all con-
ceived and planned by our heavenly Father. Soon Jesus will return in
glory and welcome us, a vast immigrant wave, into that urban home

where a place is prepared for us in the New Jerusalem, and we will be forever with Him.

Abraham looked for that city (Hebrews 11:10); so should we! There will be gathered people from every race, tribe, people, and tongue with the Body of Christ complete. My longing is to contribute to that heavenly throng by being a blessing to the immigrant nations that surround me right now.

NOTES

[1]Marilyn Ehle, "Politicians Should Be Careful," *The Gazette*, Sept. 15, 2015, www.gazette.com/letters-time-for-GOP-to-get-serious-politicians-should-be -careful/article/1559344. Scripture quotation taken from James 3:5-6, 8.

[2]Associated Press, Aug. 16, 2015.

[3]Associated Press, Sept. 15, 2015.

[4]The New York Times, front page of National Edition, June 18, 2015. The U.N. figure is for calendar 2014, counting those who left their homes due to "persecution, conflict, generalized violence, or human rights violations."

[5]Associated Press, Aug. 29, 2015.

[6]Associated Press, Sept. 16, 2015.

[7]Associated Press, Sept. 7, 2015.

[8]Associated Press, Oct. 27, 2015.

[9]Associated Press, Dec. 23, 2015.

[10]Gwladys Fouche, "Growing Number of Asylum Seekers Opt for Arctic Route to Enter Europe," *Reuters*, November 11, 2015, www.reuters.com/article/ us-europe-migrants-arctic/growing-number-of-asylum-seekers-opt-for-arctic -route-to-enter-europe-idUSKCN0T028720151111.

[11]Eve Conant, "The World's Congested Human Migration Routes in 5 Maps," *National Geographic*, September 19, 2015, https://news.nationalgeographic. com/2015/09/150919-data-points-refugees-migrants-maps-human- migrations-syria-world/.

[12]Jenny Yang, "Immigrants in the US: A Missional Opportunity," *Anthology*, May 2013, 42.

[13]Associated Press, "Today's Migrants Face More Suspicion" by Kristen Gelineau, Sept. 19, 2015.

[14]Associated Press, "Hungary Closes Border to Migrants" by Dusan Stojanovic and Vanessa Gera, Sept. 16, 2015.

[15]Associated Press, "Immigration Protest: Murrieta Latest Flashpoint in Debate," *Fox News*, July 4, 2014, www.foxnews.com/us/2014/07/04/immigration -protest-murrieta-latest-flashpoint-in-debate.html.

[16]Heather MacDonald, "Practical Thoughts on Immigration," *Imprimis*, February 2015 (vol. 44 no. 2).

[17]Pew Research Center, "40z The Growing Number of Newcomers from Other Countries Threaten Traditional American Customs and Values," *Pew Research Center*, www.people-press.org/values-questions/q40z/ newcomers-from-other-countries-threaten-traditional-american-values/#total and Michael Lipka and Jessica Martinez, "Catholics, Especially Hispanics, Echo Pope's Call to Embrace Immigrants," *Pew Research Center*, September 25, 2015, www.pewresearch.org/fact-tank/2015/09/25/ catholics-especially-hispanics-echo-popes-call-to-embrace-immigrants/.

[18]John Lantigua, "Illegal Immigrants Pay Social Security Tax, Won't Benefit," *The Seattle Times*, December 28, 2011, www.seattletimes.com/nation-world/ illegal-immigrants-pay-social-security-tax-wont-benefit/.

[19]World Migration Report 2015 (Geneva, Switzerland: International Organization for Migration), 78.

[20]National Association of Evangelicals "Webinar on the Refugee Crisis" conducted Oct. 7, 2015.

[21]Jenny Yang, "Immigrants in the U.S.: A Missional Opportunity," *Anthology*, May 2013, 42.

[22]Meira Svirsky, "German Police Warn of De Facto No-Go Zones," *Clarion Project*, August 3, 2015, https://clarionproject.org/german-police-warn -de-facto-no-go-zones-2/.

[23]E. J. Dionne, "Why welcome refugees? It's the right thing to do," op-ed page of *The Colorado Springs Gazette*, Sept. 15, 2015.

[24]Jon Clifton, "150 Million Adults Worldwide Would Migrate to the U.S.," *Gallup*, April 20, 2012, http://news.gallup.com/poll/153992/150-million -adults-worldwide-migrate.aspx.

[25]"Yemen's Neglected Disaster," *Time Magazine*, Nov. 9, 2015, pp. 38-43.

[26]"Pope Francis Urges Forgiveness in the Central African Republic." *NBC Nightly News*, November 29, 2015, www.nbcnews.com/nightly-news/video/ pope-francis-urges-forgiveness-in-the-central-african-republic-576031811701.

[27]Fraser Nelson, "Prepare yourselves: The Great Migration will be with us for decades," *Daily Telegraph*, Sept. 3, 2015.

[28]"Understanding the Migrant Crisis," *The New York Times* (International Edition), Sept. 28, 2015, p. A11.

[29]"U.N. Warns of 'Lost Generation' Deprived of School" by Rick Gladstone, *New York Times*, Sept. 3, 2015.

[30]World Watch Monitor, "A Migrant's Story," *World Watch Monitor*, August 17, 2015, www.worldwatchmonitor.org/2015/08/a-migrants-story/.

[31]Thomas Albinson, "Justice and Compassion: Responding to the Refugee Crisis in Europe," available for PDF download at www.iafr.org.

[32]"The Great Migration" special section, *TIME*, Oct. 19, 2015, p. 45.

[33]"Syrian doctor turned people smuggler" by Richard Spencer, *The Telegraph*, Sept. 20, 2015.

[34]"The Great Migration," *TIME*, p. 55.

[35]Jon Hirst, "Is Your Heart Ready to Help?" *Christianity Today*, December 10, 2015, www.christianitytoday.com/edstetzer/2015/december/is-your-heart-ready-to-help.html.

[36]Albinson, op. cit.

[37]http://wheatonbible.org/content.aspx?site_id=10713

[38]David Roller, "Heart and Sole," *Light & Life Magazine*, April 2015, pp. 7-8.

[39]Benjamin Wittes, "In Defense of Refugees" posted Nov. 17, 2015 at https://lawfareblog.com/defense-refugees.

[40]Sarah Eekhoff Zylstra, "Christians Debate State Bans on Syrian Refugees after Paris Attacks," *Christianity Today*, November 17, 2015, http://www.christianitytoday.com/news/2015/november/christians-debate-state-bans-syrian-refugees-paris-attacks.html.

[41]Ibid.

[42]Joseph Castleberry, *The New Pilgrims: How Immigrants Are Renewing America's Faith and Values* (Nashville: Worthy, 2015), p. 3.

[43]Interview with Kelly Wright on the program *America's News HQ*, Oct. 26, 2015.

[44]John Stossel, "Immigration Is Good; Just Consider the Facts," *The Gazette* (Aug. 14, 2015), p. A13.

[45]Paul Borthwick, "Western Christian in Global Mission," *Anthology*, May 2013, pp. 60-61.

[46]Ibid.

[47]Trevin Wax, "Why Evangelicals Are Torn About Admitting Refugees to the US," *Religion News Service*, November 18, 2015, http://religionnews.com/2015/11/18/evangelicals-torn-admitting-refugees-us-analysis/.

[48]Ibid.

[49]Albinson, op. cit.

[50]Tass Saada with Dean Merrill, *The Mind of Terror* (Carol Stream, Ill.: Tyndale, 2016), chap. 2

[51]Thomas K. Johnson, "Xenophobia, Hospitality, and the Refugee Crisis in Europe," posted at http://worldea.org/news/4599/xenophobia-hospitality-and -the-refugee-crisis-in-Europe.

[52]J. Kwabena Asamoah-Gyadu, "Migration, Diaspora Mission, and Religious Others in World Christianity: An African Perspective," International Bulletin of Missionary Research (Vol. 39, No. 4—Oct. 2015), 191.

[53]Asamoah-Gyadu, op. cit, 190.

[54]Tass Saada with Dean Merrill, *The Mind of Terror* (Carol Stream, Ill.: Tyndale, 2016), chap. 12.

[55]Katelyn Beaty and Skye Jethani, "Meanwhile, Love the Sojourner," *Christianity Today*, September 6, 2012, http://www.christianitytoday.com/ct/2012/ september/meanwhile-love-sojourner.html.

[56]Ibid.

[57]Christian Aid Mission, "Refugees from Syria, Iraq Seek Help to Survive," *Christian Aid Mission*, December 17, 2015, http://www.christianaid.org/ News/2015/mir20151217.aspx.

[58]Joanne Appleton, "Supporting Church-Planting in Migrant Communities," ECPN Concept Paper 8, European Church-Planting Network, 2010, http:// ministryformation.com.au/attachments/article/177/supporting_church_ planting.pdf.

[59]Bradley Wright, "Dear Pastor, Can I Come to Your Church?" *Christianity Today*, July 21, 2015, www.christianitytoday.com/ct/2015/july-august/dear-pastor-can-i-come-to-your-church.html. For the full research report, see *Journal for the Scientific Study of Religion*, June 2015 issue.

[60]Kirsten Grieshaber, "At a Berlin Church, Muslim Refugees Converting in Droves," *Associated Press*, September 4, 2015, https://apnews.com/0550c 14ba3024c06820218f79bc6cf07/berlin-church-muslim-refugees-converting-droves.

[61]Appleton, op. cit.

[62]Wright, op. cit., p. 34

[63] Appleton, op. cit.

[64] James Watson, "Contextualization and Interaction Mapping," *Christianity Today*, October 2015, www.christianitytoday.com/edstetzer/channel/utilities/print.html?type-article&id=131810.

[65] https://paoc.org/missions/global-view/articles/god-is-doing-a-new-thing-refugees-want-to-know-who-is-isa-almasih-%28jesus-christ%29

[66] Melody Wachsmuth, "The Refugee Crisis Frontline: Croatia's Christians Lend a Hand," *Christianity Today*, September 22, 2015, www.christianitytoday.com/ct/channel/utilities/print.html?type=article&id=131661.

[67] "Closing remarks as delivered," High Commissioner's Dialogue on Protection Challenges, Theme: Faith and Protection (12-13 December 2012), Antonio Guterres, United Nations High Commissioner for Refugees.

[68] GC2 Summit Declaration, "Christian Declaration on Caring for Refugees: An Evangelical Response," GC2 Summit, www.reconciliationjusticenetwork.com/wp-content/uploads/2016/02/GC2-Summit-Declaration.pdf.

[69] http://iafr.org/downloads/handouts/5%20Reasons%20Followers%20of%20Christ%20Seek%20the%20Protection%20and%20Welfare%20of%20Refugees.pdf

[70] Elizabeth Kendal, "RLPB 326. Christian Crisis in the Middle East," Religious Liberty Prayer Bulletin, September 9, 2015, http://rlprayerbulletin.blogspot.com/2015/09/rlpb-326-christian-crisis-in-middle-east.html.

[71] http://www.desiringgod.org/articles/building-his-church-in-a-refugee-crisis, posted Nov. 19, 2015.

ALSO AVAILABLE

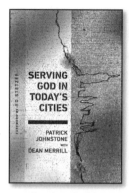

**Serving God in
Today's Cities**
978-0-8308-4536-1

**The Future of the
Global Church**
978-0-8308-5695-4

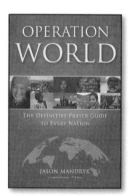

Operation World
978-0-8308-5824-1

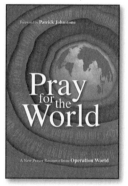

Pray for the World
978-0-8308-3686-4

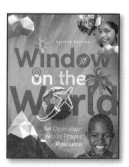

Window on the World
978-0-8308-5783-8